ACKNC

MW01609775

With enormous gratitude I acknowledge the following for their invaluable assistance in completing this book:

Sterling Dunn, Sales Supervisor, Branded-New England Co.
Daniel Michaud, Sales Manager, Ruby Wines, Inc.
Shawn Ford, Vice President, Historic Tours of America
Soteiria Minasidis, my research assistant
Mark Olezek
Joan Smoller
Roseanne Mercer
Pat Wagoner
John Mayo
Bill Ferrall
Al Lynch
Christine Albrecht
Joyce Jordan, Sales Manager, Alternative Solutions Inc.
Judith Pike, my daughter the lawyer
Laurence Pike, my son the nite owl and financial wizard
Karen Pike, my daughter the photo/journalist
Loretta McGovern, my business partner
Cathy Beyer, my computer instructor
Donna, my hairdresser from Shear Excitement, who made me look good
Phyllis Shapiro, whose hospitality revived me to write again

Dedicated to

J. Edward Cambron,
my life partner whose belief in me is unwavering

I

INTRODUCTION

"I have just returned from Boston.
It is the only sane thing to do if you find yourself up there."

Fred Allen in a 1953 letter to Groucho Marx

The perception about "staid, conservative Boston" unjustifiably lives on. Its emergence from the dark ages has, thusfar, been among the best-kept secrets in the world. Pike's Peek at Boston By Night finally reveals that Boston is as exciting and inviting by night as by day. Pike's Peak at Boston By Night is uniquely different from any other city resource book. Not only is it a comprehensive guide dedicated exclusively to Boston's nightlife, but it is written by a lifelong resident who has first-hand knowledge of every nook and all of the city's crannies.

What separates ...Boston By Night even more from other guidebooks is the inclusion of adequate details necessary to make an informed decision as to whether one would enjoy a particular restaurant or club and whether it is appropriate to one's tastes or lifestyle. For each listing there is a review of what one can expect upon arrival such as type and age of clientele, if there is a dress code, the style and quality of the food and service, if there is valet or validated parking and how much, decor and ambience, type of music and entertainment, if any, and if there is dancing. All of this in addition to the basic information contained in each listing, no referring back to confusing codes and graphs. This includes hours, price range, whether reservations and credit cards are accepted and extent of bar service.

Listing all of Boston's restaurants, bars, clubs, cafes, pubs, and taverns as well as the plethora of other nocturnal activities would require a book too heavy to tote for easy reference. Therefore, the suggestions contained herein are a microcosm of the off-beat, outre, trendy, ethnic, elegant and inexpensive of sufficient variety to please even the most committed carouser. The focus is on what's hot, what's fun, what's different, as well as on best buys and the lavish worth hocking the farm for rather than on the cornerstones of the city's dining and entertainment experiences listed in other publications. However, any book that presumes to be a Boston guide would be remiss in not at least mentioning some of these sentimental favorites, so I will.

Included are restaurants and clubs, entertainment centers such as bowling alleys, pool halls and miniature golf courses, all listed by geographic locations, as well as 24-hour markets, drug stores, gas stations, and other all-night services. The information was gathered by personal encounters (a ten-pound experience), by picking the brains of friends in-the-know, by following purveyors of food and spirits (they're like hairdressers—everyone tells them their secrets), ditto bartenders, and by accosting strangers who were willing to share evaluations of their nightly jaunts through Boston. A separate page in the back of the book gives information about Boston's Rapid Transit System, The "T," with a map marked to show which stops on which lines are within the districts mentioned, and other transportation services.

...Boston By Night is the ideal resource for anyone who wants to be more in-the-know about where to go and what to do in Boston after the sun goes down, anyone who wants to get the best and the most out of a city that has leaped into world-class status over the last two decades. This includes tourists, convention and seminar participants, the 200,000-plus students who descend on Boston each fall, residents who want to expand their knowledge of the city, and self-exiled suburbanites who have thusfar been reluctant to explore the city without better guidelines. After reading ...Boston By Night, no one could ever again regard the term "Boston nightlife" as an oxymoron.

PREFACE

Boston came by its nocturnally deprived reputation honestly. For generations the city's code of behavior had been dictated by the Puritan precepts drafted by Reverend Samuel Peters in the seventeenth century known as the "Blue Laws," reputedly so named for the color of the parchment on which they were printed. In those days, it was even against the law for a woman to kiss her child on the Sabbath. Although these laws declined after the American Revolution, many were revived in the twentieth century during prohibition and remained on Massachusetts' books for several decades.

The Blue Laws were focused on protecting the Christian Sabbath, "the common day of rest that shall include the time from midnight Saturday to midnight Sunday," but the mindset extended throughout the week. Everything was shut tight by midnight, certainly on the weekend, even earlier on week nights. Boston was not known for its nightlife. In fact, it was known for not having a nightlife, perhaps true in the 1960's and most of the '70s but a bum rap for the two decades prior to that.

Despite the curfew and the propensity of the population, clubs proliferated in the '40s and '50s. Some of the best jazz musicians, pop singers and comedians cut their teeth on Boston audiences in such clubs as Steuben's, Blinstrub's and the High Hat. These clubs and the ilk of performers they featured died when rock and roll was born. Concert halls and arenas that could hold thousands of screaming fans replaced the glamour and sophistication of these bistros that could accommodate only a minute fraction of that number.

By the middle of the 1960's when music tastes had changed radically and social standards were redefined, the natives were getting restless. Legislators were finally convinced that the Blue Laws had to be relaxed, but their constituents' campaigns for a more permissive society or their arguments that these laws flaunted federal mandate dictating the separation of church and state had little to do with the repeals. Money was the great motivator. Tourism as an industry was suffering badly, in large part due to Boston's archaic laws. Travelers from more lenient societies (which were just about anywhere other than Massachusetts) viewed Boston as a quick stop-over to conduct business and/or to take a fast historic tour. They were accustomed to starting their nights at 10 or 11 p.m. and a midnight curfew was a joke. Few hung around any longer than they had to to spread their wealth.

"Girls (and Boys) Just Want to Have Fun" became the marching song for most of the free world, and the newly liberated Bostonians joined in, but they wanted it on their own turf. The real turning point for Boston's revitalization came in the 1970's when former Mayor Kevin White pushed through a waterfront development project. It changed the face and the attitude of the city. Known as Quincy Market, it serves as the prototype for similar projects in several cities across the country and as the paragon for city rejuvination.

Like the rats blithely following the soulful sounds of the Pied Piper's flute, financial backers responded to Boston's new tune. Before long there were clubs springing up all over the city offering everything from comedy to miniature golf and from blues to heavy metal. Bostonians began to get back at their nocturnal deprivation with a vengeance. Now, nightlife is embraced with the same fanaticism that created the Blue Laws. Throughout the city, residents and their suburban cousins are trading in their once favorite form of entertainment, house parties, for the city's myriad delights.

Liquor, still, cannot legally pass a customer's lips past 2 a.m., but as the sadistic interrogator said to his cringing prisoner, "We have our ways." After-hours clubs, long a New York cachet, proliferate now in Boston as well, but not quite so overtly. Penalties for revealing locations or even the existence thereof could include ostracism, harrassment, even physical injury, possibly all of the above. Qualification for entering, given that one could unearth locations, follow the prohibition-speakeasy pattern of a human mountain peering through a peephole to determine if one speaks the truth when reporting "Joe sent me." Those that show up at the door are usually pretty confident of gaining admission. After all, no one wants to fool with "Mother Mountain."

That "private" party going on in homes and apartments across the city in the middle of the night may in fact be public. Guests pay to get in and probably have never met the host before. Where and when these parties take place are known only to those who know someone who know someone, and so on. Locations and hosts change on a regular basis, something like a floating crap game without the dice.

The latest rave in Boston is just that—"The Rave." Originating in

Europe, raves begin there after midnight and last until dawn, generally outdoors on the fringes of the city. Boston has a more limited version, beginning anywhere from 10 p.m. to midnight, ending at 2 a.m., and indoors. Several of Boston's clubs take turns catering to "ravers." Music is generally Eurodisco and clientele is primarily Middle Eastern, European and South American who prefer the more ethnic music and crowds. Many are in Boston attending universities and are incredibly wealthy. Some have been known to use bottles of Moet Chandon as spray guns to attract attention.

Whether they know it or not, these students have participated in the dousing of the fire and brimstone that sparked three hundred years of restrictive living. Though a few "Blue Laws" tenaciously cling to the books, they are just about history. Some Boston natives put this on the same miraculous level as the dismantling of the Berlin Wall and the dissolution of the Soviet Union. The new breed asks "Why did it take so long?"

"And this is good old Boston, the home of the bean and the cod,
Where the Lowells talk to the Cabots and the Cabots talk only to God."
John Collins Bossidy in a toast at a 1910 Holy Cross Alumni Dinner

The Fred Allen and John Bossidy observations chiding Boston's rigidity and dearth of diversions were fairly accurate when made five and eight decades ago. Ah, if old Fred and John could see us now. As the ad says, "We've come a long way, baby."

TABLE OF CONTENTS

TABLE OF CONTENTS

As of this writing, there are 2,169 licensed eating and drinking establishments operating in the City of Boston, and the number keeps growing. No wonder that someone unfamiliar with the city is so bewildered and tends to return to the few tried-and-true rather than experiment. Without adequate back-up information, experimentation can be disappointing and expensive. The listings here paint enough of a picture to make the daunted dauntless and are set up geographically so that you know where you are going before you start out and if you want to be there. Unless otherwise specified, all of the restaurants accept reservations and credit cards, have full liquor licenses, and do not offer valet or validated parking. Those preceded by * serve food after midnight (even if only pizza or pastries and coffee); those with ** are strictly vegetarian. Since this book is about Boston By Night, only the dinner hours are specified for those restaurants that close between lunch and dinner.

BACK BAY

Once totally under water, the Back Bay was on the drawing board for over 40 years and is Boston's only planned section where streets are in a grid. Running east and west, Boylston and Newbury are the two principal commerical streets with cross streets named alphabetically from Arlington to Ipswich. Newbury Street is Boston's answer to Rodeo Drive, at least the first five blocks. The rest, known as Lower Newbury (with the emphasis on Lower) did not enjoy the same prestige until recently when funky shops and swanky restaurants were opened, breathing new, stylish life into the area. At the southern edge of Back Bay is Copley Place, the largest private development in Boston, covering almost 10 acres of shops, hotels, restaurants, a cinema, residences and parking garage. Located between Boylston Street and Huntington Avenue is a revived Prudential Center also with shops and restaurants, a food court, and hotel. The Skywalk Observation Deck on the 50th floor of the Prudential Tower is in renovation as of this writing and is scheduled to reopen with new amenities in mid September, 1994. The entrance price will be increased from $3.75 to around $5, according to the new owners,

American

*Sonsie, 327 Newbury St, 351-2500
7 a.m.-1 a.m. daily; valet parking $8
If stealing the thunder from other Back Bay restaurants was a punishable offense, Sonsie's owner would have been arrested on the first day it opened (winter '94); undeniably Boston's hottest of the current hot spots where the sleek blend harmoniously with the grunge. The eclectic menu offers something for everyone whether a "nosh" or a meal; entrees average $20, but you can fill up on a soup and a salad for around $15; decor is a cacophony of Moroccan, European and '50s/'60s kitsch (the ladies' room is papered with covers from a now-defunct, '60s gossip rag).

29 Newbury, 29 Newbury St, 536-0290
5 p.m.-11 p.m. Mon-Sat, to 9 p.m. Sun, lunch also served
The showcase for the eminently well groomed and stylish where the less fashion conscious are not exactly welcomed with open arms by the snooty servers and clientele; seasonal menu; food unpredictable (sometimes great, sometimes not); small (probably to keep out the riff raff), intimate (mostly booth seating); sidewalk cafe (in season) is one of the best for rubber necking; moderately priced, although a full dinner for two with the de rigueur two pre-meal martinis and wine with, could approach the price of a low-end Armani tie - about $125.

Library Grill, 84 Beacon St (in the Hampshire House), 227-9600
5 p.m.-10:15 p.m. daily; valet parking $8
Like dining in the library of someone's elegant townhouse, which it was; turn-of-the-century charm complete with wood-panelled walls, crystal chandeliers and working marble fireplace; good seafood and duck, its specialties, $16-$19; live music in adjoining lounge; have a pre- or post-dinner drink in the famed "Cheers" Bar (The Bull & Finch Pub) located in the basement.

*Dick's Last Resort, 55 Huntington Ave, 267-8080
11 a.m.-2 a.m. daily; validated parking at adjoining garage;
no reservations Fri & Sat
Devoid of any class and proud of it - that's the whole idea here; finger-licking foods served in buckets with squares of butcher paper doubling as

your place setting (what do you expect at these prices?); even the desserts are messy, mainly fudgey and gooey. To put you right at home, servers are bossy, and tables are shared; decor early playroom gone wild - neon beer signs and Elvis on velvet; enough kinds of beer to taste a new brand 75 nights in a row; live music seven nights.

Original Sports Saloon, 47 Huntington Ave (in the Copley Square Hotel), 536-1904
11:30 a.m.-2 a.m. (dinner to 10, appetizers to midnight); reservations for 10 or more
A sports fan's paradise, especially one who likes to chomp on award winning barbecued ribs and chicken while watching a game on large-screen satellite TVs; $5-$9; fascinating, authentic sports memorabilia; home of 30 college alumnis and hangout for the sports media.

*Hard Rock Cafe, 131 Clarendon St, 424-7625
11 a.m-2 a.m; food to midnight Sun-Thurs, to 1 a.m. Fri & Sat
Mentioned primarily to boast that Boston is an important enough city to have one of these international Rock 'n Roll Halls of Fame/Restaurants; a place to see if you haven't seen one and the place to be if you like burgers and barbecue surrounded by rock 'n roll memorabilia and thunderous music. Crowd varies from teenagers to tourists who generally can be counted on to increase Hard Rock revenues in the adjacent souvenir shop.

Other Side Cafe, 407 Newbury St, 536-9477
10 a.m.-midnight Mon-Sat, opens at noon on Sun; no reservations; cash only
You have to cross Mass. Ave to get to this part of Newbury St. where there is little else but a parking lot and a garage. Typical cafe foods ($1-$14), but the fresh-squeezed juices are a big draw; loft above the cafe is reminiscent of a college dorm room with mismatched couches and coffee tables (to put its principal clientele in familiar surroundings, no doubt); large, outside, raised deck (in season) gives an unhampered view of the Mass Turnpike and Tower Records; live jazz band Sundays, times vary but always after 3 p.m.

Asian

Mr. Leung, 595 Boylston St, 236-4040
Noon-10 pm. Mon-Fri, 5-11 p.m. Sat, to 10 p.m. Sun; valet parking $9
Below street level but a step above what most expect from Chinese
dining - elegant surroundings, fine food and white-glove treatment; also
a step up (or two or three) in cost - entrees range from $18-$24; lounge is
a lively pre-club gathering place for the International set. A more moderately priced "Mr. Leung," named **"Eurosia,"** located in The Boston Park
Plaza Hotel on Arlington Street, opened late April '94 (see **LATE ENTRIES**
at end of **RESTAURANT** listings).

Continental

Biba, 272 Boylston St. 426-7878
11:30 a.m.-1 a.m. daily; valet parking $10 (day), $9 (night)
Owned by a world-renowned chef, and her restaurant lives up to her
fame. Bistro atmosphere and food on first floor, more formal dining on
the second; high end of moderate heading toward expensive; lively bar -
another of the many nightly stops made by Boston's very mobile BP's
(beautiful people).

Ritz-Carlton Hotel, 15 Arlington St, 536-5700
Dining Room, 5:30 p.m.-10 p.m. Sun-Thurs, to 11 Fri & Sat
Everything it's cracked up to be and then some; spectacular view of
Boston Public Garden to match the spectacular food and unequaled
service; a dining experience, complete with live piano music, worth sacrific-
ing a week's worth of grocery shopping, and you may have to.
Cafe, 6:30 a.m.-midnight daily
Just as "Ritzy" and delightful but not as expensive - entrees $18 and under.
Rooftop, 6 p.m.-1 a.m. Fri & Sat in season
Dine and dance al fresco to live swing and contemporary music.
Jackets for the gentlemen in all rooms, please; patrons are generally
elegantly dressed - putting on the Ritz, so to speak.

French

L'Espalier, 30 Gloucester St, 262-3023
6 p.m.-10 p.m. Mon-Sat; valet parking $10; reservations urged
Magnifique immediately comes to mind when describing this gracious
restaurant as Parisian as the Champs Élysées; fresh New England ingredients prepared in flawless French contemporary; ever-changing prix-fixe
menu ($56 pp); 250 wine selections; an elegant setting that deserves the
jacket and tie requested.

DuBarry, 159 Newbury St., 262-2445;
Validated parking in adjoining lot $3
5:30 p.m. to 10 p.m. Mon-Sat, to 9:30 Sun; also serves lunch
This family owned, old-style classic French restaurant may have fallen out
of favor with the chic, but other French restaurants have yet to touch the
genious of its rabbit with peas and pearl onions in mustard; the glass-
enclosed terrace affords a nice view without any of the street fumes.

Grills

Grill 23, 161 Berkeley St, 542-2255
6 p.m.-10:30 p.m. Mon-Thurs, to 11 Fri & Sat, 6-10 Sun; valet parking $7
Among the most grand and stately dining rooms in the city; noted for its
steaks and seafood, but the lamb and veal are equally delectable.
Forget the diet and go for the garlic mashed potatoes - worth every
calorie and gram of fat; an extensive, international wine list and killer
martinis; brush off the little black dress to fit right in this elegant but not-
too-showy setting.

Capital Grille, 359 Newbury St, 262-8900
5 p.m.-10 p.m. Mon-Thurs, to 11:30 Fri & Sat, to 10:30 Sun
Bar to midnight, earlier on slow nights; valet parking $7
The power plant of lower Newbury St. until Sonsie came along to steal
some of its energy but still among the best and most "in" places in town; a
New York-style steak house offering fish and poultry as well; a la carte
entrees range from $14-$25; luxurious surroundings and special perks such as

phone service at each table (for the few who don't carry their own) and private wine storage bins for regular patrons, most of whom can well afford them.

Morton's, 1 Exeter Pl, 266-5858
5:30 p.m.-11 p.m. Mon-Sat, to 10 Sun; lunch Mon-Fri
Sort of stuck in the '80's where "the suits" spend a lot of time power dining on generous expense accounts, mainly on the house specialty—a 24-ounce porterhouse (that's how you feed a hungry man); $19-$30; a "clubby" atmosphere where men may be allowed to loosen their ties but not remove them (nor their jackets).

Hungarian

Cafe Budapest, 90 Exeter St (in the Copley Square Hotel), 266-1979
5 p.m.-10:30 p.m. Sun-Thurs, to midnight Fri & Sat; also serves lunch
Parking in Copley Place across the street
The quintessential quantum leap back to pre-World-War-II Hungary. Starched, glowing white table linens can't outshine the tuxedoed waiters who coddle you as if they were transported to work in a time machine. Rated best in its category for a quarter century. Flaming crepes suzette, a strolling violinist and a pianist (who can't stroll) heighten the romantic atmosphere. Adding to the glamour is owner Dr. Livia Hedda Rev-Kury holding court nightly, always dressed in white. All this does not come cheap - average entree around $30.

Indian

Kashmir, 279 Newbury St., 536-1695
11:30 a.m.- 11 p.m. Mon-Fri, opens at noon Sat & Sun; valet parking $8
This place curries favor with diners yearning for authentic Tandori-style Indian cooking; entrees $9-$18; so sari, oops, sorry - only soft drinks.

International

Small Planet Bar & Grill, 565 Boylston St, 536-4477
5 p.m.-10 p.m. Sun & Mon, to 10:30 Tues-Sat, appetizer menu to midnight
Bar open to 1 a.m. nightly; reservations only for 8 or more

Global "Peasant Cuisine" (paella, curries, stir fry, pizzas, etc.) at plebian prices fit for the peerage yet cozy and inviting to the masses; 10 percent of pre-tax profit is donated to the Boston Food Bank and Oxfam.

Wire House, 20 Park Plaza, 292-0527
7 a.m.-midnight daily; no reservations; just beer & wine
News junkies can indulge their passion even while eating at this recently opened (April, '94) "media cafe." While "global grazing" (the restaurant's term for its tasting menu format), diners may skim through some 400 international newspapers and magazines and watch one of several televisions tuned in to CNN. In addition to a core menu, there are special selections that will change according to the news. One can only hope they concentrate on the positive news and not settle for such "downers" as "Whitewater shrimp" or "Bosnian barbecued ribs." Curved around the end of the Statler Building, it is mainly windowed, hence bright and open. However, the chairs (uncomfortable) and tables, chosen to effect someone's perception of European decor, would fit more properly in an ice cream parlor.

Italian

Emporio Armani Express, 214 Newbury St., 437-0909
11:30 a.m.-1 a.m. daily (food served to midnight)
Valet parking $8; no reservations in first-floor cafe
Don't let the name scare you - the cafe is moderately priced (about $35 for two) or you can opt for the pre-theatre (5-7 p.m), prix fixe, three-course dinner at $25 pp.; authentic Northern Italian dishes; loud, exciting, pulsating and sophisticated with Euro/Latino background music by day and agressive club music by night. The ristorante offers same style food but more refined and so is the atmosphere. Plan on $75-$100 unless you go bare bones. Jackets for the gentlemen preferred here but they won't throw you out in your shirtsleeves. Large Euro/Latino clientele but Bostonians have found a home there as well.

Rocco's, 5 Charles St. South, 723-6800
5 p.m-10 p.m. Sun-Tues, to 10:30 Wed & Thurs, to 11 p.m. Fri & Sat, open for lunch
Valet parking Tues-Sat $8; reservations strongly suggested

Amiable, artistic, comfortable and large but warm; tasty regional Italian food for $60-$70 for two; may be where those with real panache congregate.

Papa Razzi, 271 Dartmouth St., 536-9200
11:30 a.m.-10 p.m. (11 for pizza) Sun-Wed, to 11 Thurs-Sat (midnight for pizza); Bar open to 2 a.m.; valet parking $6
Nothing exceptional about the food and service, but most notable as one of the favored watering holes for the "in" people; Italian nouvelle at moderate prices.

La Famiglia Giorgio's, 250 Newbury St., 247-1569
11 a.m.-10:30 p.m. daily
Everyone who has eaten here has the same thing to say: "cheap, good and monster portions;" service is fast paced (though friendly) so the inevitable line goes quickly; another, larger restaurant in the North End at 112 Salem St, 367-6711 (also in Brookline and East Boston).

Davio's, 269 Newbury St, 262-4810
5 p.m.-11 p.m. Mon-Sun; valet parking $8
Gracious dining on excellent Northern Italian cuisine, less formally and less expensively ($9-$15) in the upstairs cafe and more elegantly and costly ($15-$25) downstairs where there is no smoking and gentlemen are expected to dress as gentlemen (jackets); two others at 202 Washington St, Brookline Village, 738-4810, and in The Royal Sonesta Hotel, 5 Cambridge Parkway, Cambridge, 661-4810

Japanese

*Gyuhama, 827 Boylston St, 437-0188
Noon to 2 a.m. daily; no reservations
Loud and expensive but different; a favorite with the young, hip Japanese Bostonian crowd who favor the "rock 'n roll" sushi. Sail into the "Happy Boat"- it's varied and tantalizing if you like raw fish.

Miyako, 279A Newbury St, 236-0222
Noon-10:30 p.m. Sun-Thurs, to 11 Fri & Sat; reservations for 3 or more
Papa is in the kitchen, and mama is in the dining room guaranteeing that

food is authentic and service is in honorable Japanese tradition; reasonably priced ($5-$15); pleasant, contemporary atmosphere.

Seafood

Legal Sea Foods, 20 Park Plaza (in the Boston Park Plaza Hotel) 426-4444; Free valet parking after 5 p.m.; Also in Prudential Centre 266-6800, and Copley Place, 266-7775, validated garage parking ($2) after 5 p.m.; no reservations 11 a.m-10 p.m. Mon-Thurs, to 11 Fri & Sat, noon-10 p.m. Sun
A legend in its own time for the freshest, purest seafood available this side of the water, guaranteed by tests of the daily catch in Legal's own lab. Its rich, creamy clam chowder is in a class by itself and has been served at the last five Presidential Inaugural Dinners. Moderately priced except for the giant lobster when they're not plentiful (most of the time); enormously popular with locals and tourists alike; have a snack before you go— chances are you will have a long wait to be seated.

Skipjack's, 199 Clarendon St, 536-3500
Two hours free parking in adjacent garage
11 a.m.-10 p.m. Mon-Thurs, to 11 Fri & Sat, to 9 Sun
Fresh seafood for reasonable prices ($9-$19) in a casual, comfortable atmosphere; outdoor cafe in season; New Orleans jazz brunch on Sundays; two other locations - 2 Brookline Pl, Brookline and 5 Bennett St., Cambridge (Harvard Square).

Tex/Mex

Cottonwood Cafe, 222 Berkeley St., 247-2225
5:45 p.m.-10 p.m. Sun-Thurs, to 11 p.m. on Fri & Sat, open for lunch
Valet parking $7 or validated garage parking for 3 hrs
The Milagro bean fields are working overtime to supply the main ingredient in the black bean soup, a Cafe specialty, and the sun never seems to set on the popularity of its Tequilla Sunrise Salmon; food is hot and so is the crowd, mostly 30-something professionals whose tolerance for the multi-flavored margaritas is mythical; prices range from $12-$18 not counting the margaritas, but who's counting?

BOSTON BY NIGHT

Cactus Club, 939 Boylston St, 236-0200
5 p.m.-11 p.m. Mon-Wed, to 11:30 Thurs, to 12 Fri & Sat, to 10:30 Sun
Reservations only for groups of 8 or more
Like a Mexican bean, always jumping, mainly with a youthful, animated
crowd slurping down fruit-blended margaritas and other forms of creative
firewater; New Mexican appetizers and entrees as well as more traditional southwestern fare; filling appetizers start at $4, entrees at $14.

Rattlesnake Bar & Grille, 384 Boylston St, 859-8555
11:30 a.m.-2 a.m. daily
Slither down here primarily for its margaritas and tequila, its specialties;
food is even further south than Mexico - Central America (they eat there,
too, between coup d'etats); reasonable prices; casual, local, generally
'20s/'30s crowd.

Casa Romero, 30 Gloucester St. 536-4341
5 p.m.-10 p.m. Sun-Thurs, to 11 Fri & Sat
Free 1-hour parking at 341 Newbury St ($1 2nd hour)
Cisco Kid and his sidekick Pancho would feel right at home here; south-of-
the-border dishes and the decor (low ceilings, heavy wooden beams,
white-and-blue ceramic tiles and ladder-back mission chairs) truly bring
Old Mexico to Back Bay; as any Mexican restaurant worth its serape, they
make their own salsa and chips; renowned for its margaritas.

BEACON HILL

Time has almost stood still for Beacon Hill. The narrow, steep streets, some
still cobblestoned, with tightly packed Federalist red brick homes, have
barely changed since colonial days. Perched at the top of the Hill is the
State House and at the base, Charles Street, lined with antique, jewelry
and gift shops, art galleries and trendy little cafes.

American

Publik House, 6 Beacon St, 523-3391
11:30 a.m-11 p.m. Mon-Fri, only lunch on Sat
Good pub food cheap, generous drinks, friendly atmosphere, five TVs to

keep an eye on what's happening in the world, and plenty of political talk (this is State House country).

Chinese

*Shangri-La, 138 Cambridge St, 523-6526
11:30 a.m.-2 a.m daily; $10 minimum for credit cards
A melange of Cantonese and Szechuan dishes principally catering to American palates; baked-on-premise Chinese and French pastries also sold to go in its adjoining bakery; a la Shangri-La, a little bit of paradise awaits in their tropical drinks.

French

Hungry I, 71 Charles St, 227-3524
6-9 p.m. Sun-Thurs, to 10 Fri & Sat
If venison is your meat, and game is your game, this is the place; entrees range from $18-$26; tiny, appealing to stylishly dressed couples looking for an intimate, romantic setting.

Italian

Black Goose, 21 Beacon St, 720-4500
11:30 a.m.-10 p.m. Mon-Wed, to 11 Thurs-Sat
Just a few steps away from the State House and in the thick of a lot of politicians making decisions over plates of calamari and pasta or a pizza; the home-baked Brushetta is a real treat; jazz pianist Thurs, Fri, Sat.

The Charles Restaurant, 75 Chestnut St, 523-4477
5 p.m.-10 p.m. Mon-Thurs, to 11 Fri & Sat, to 10 on Sun; valet parking $5
Almost 50 years old and on its way to becoming a Boston landmark restaurant; consistent, good food (Northern Italian specialties) and service; entrees from $8-$22; clientele very Beacon Hill - quiet, reserved (but relaxed) and "mature;" romantic setting, particularly in one of the two private booths. The Labadinis, the owners, treat everyone as guests at a dinner party in their own home.

BOSTON BY NIGHT

Ristorante Toscano, 47 Charles St, 723-4090
11:30 a.m.-11 p.m. Mon-Sat, opens at 5:30 Sun; valet parking $7. AE or cash
Wonderful Florentine cuisine in Northern Italian ambience; entrees $7.50-
$22; jeans allowed only when worn with jackets and no tee shirts; just beer
and wine.

Thai

King & I, 145 Charles St, 227-3320
5 p.m.-9:45 p.m. Sun-Thurs, to 10:45 Fri & Sat, open for lunch
The "Pad Thai" (rice noodles with shrimp, chicken, eggs, tofu, sweet radish,
fish sauce, bean sprouts, sugar and vinegar) has Thai-ed up the "Creme
de la Creme Award" for several years; cozy, casual and reasonably
priced; just beer and wine.

Bangkok Seafood Restaurant, 26 Charles St, 723-5939
5 p.m.-10 p.m. Mon-Thurs & Sun, to 10:30 Fri & Sat
If you're hooked on tangy, exotic seafood, this is the place to drop your
line; $6-$14; just beer and wine.

BRIGHTON/ALLSTON/BROOKLINE

Just a few miles outside of the city's center, Brighton and Allston are
havens to those seeking citified life at lower housing costs. Given the
proximity of these areas to Boston's numerous colleges and universities,
students constitute a large part of the population as well. The desirability
of these fringe communities is enhanced by easy, quick access downtown
by public transportation. A bit more affluent, Brookline is a separate
township, included here only to list those establishments that are worth
traveling for (10-15 minutes from downtown Boston) or are unique to the
area. For example, anyone who strictly adheres to Jewish dietary laws
must go to Brookline to dine out since there is only one kosher restaurant
in downtown Boston (Milk Street Cafe) and it's open only from 7 a.m. to 3
p.m. A profusion of other restaurants and clubs, some unlike anything
found in the core city (which we will focus on), cater to these heterogeneous communities and to hordes of visitors from other neighborhoods.
After all, the "easy, quick" public transportation goes both ways.

Asian

Hanmiok, 351 Washington St, Brighton, 783-2090 (Japanese/Korean)
11:30 a.m.-11 p.m. Mon-Wed, to 11:30 Thurs-Sun
Unassuming in structure and ambience but commanding in the excellent,
authentic food it serves up daily at very reasonable prices; highest ticket
item is the special Sushi box for $30, enough for two but often scoffed
down by one, very hungry, very happy eater; large Japanese/Korean
clientele which tells its own story.

Pho Pasteur, 137 Brighton Ave, Allston, 783-2340 (Vietnamese)
11 a.m.-11 p.m. Mon-Sat, to 10 Sun
Getting in the soup doesn't mean trouble here - it's the way to go, right to
the Pho (Vietnamese noodle soup) or one of the other piping hot broths
filled with your choice of ingredients, a delicious, satisfying meal for around
$4; an enormous selection of other dishes range from $3-$8.

San Francisco Noodle House, 1029 Comm. Ave (just past B.U.), 783-5111
11:30 a.m-10 p.m. Sun-Thurs, to 11:30 Fri & Sat
Good, basic Chinese food cheap; oodles of noodles from chow mein to lo
mein, most under $5; student crowd and locals who can't eat this cheap at home.

Shalom Hunan, 92 Harvard St, Brookline, 731-9778
See **Kosher** listing in this section.

**Shang Chai Delight Vegetarian Restaurant, 404A Harvard St,
Brookline, 232-2424; See **Kosher** listing in this section.

Brazilian

Cafe Brazil, 421 Cambridge St, Allston, 789-5980
11:30 a.m.-10 p.m. 7 days; reservations for parties of four or more
Only the Rio de Janeiro travel posters give any hint that this prosaic,
store-front restaurant is Brazilian until you taste the food - good in a simple,
authentic way - and if you happen to hit a night when a guitarist is strum-
ming Federative Republic favorites; the abundance of Portuguese-speaking
patrons testify to its authenticity; moderately priced; just beer and wine.

International

Harvard Street Grill, 398 Harvard St, Brookline, 734-9834
5:30 p.m.-9 p.m. Tues-Thurs, to 10 Fri & Sat
One of those "best kept secrets" that has recently been discovered;
limited, ever-changing menu, extremely fresh, very well prepared and
artfully presented. Chef/owner is a Ritz Carlton alumnus which, in itself,
attests to his talents, but his restaurant is a tad too pricey for its portions
and small, storefront, suburban location, easily $70-$80 for two with
appetizer OR dessert, and wine; just beer and wine.

Italian

Providence, 1223 Beacon St, Brookline, 232-0300
5:30 p.m.-10 p.m. Tues-Thurs, to 11 p.m. Fri & Sat, 5-9 p.m. Sun; valet parking $5
With all the great Italian restaurants in the North End, why travel to
Brookline, you may ask? Because it's worth it! This is a true dining experience as it was meant to be - the chairs are comfortable, patrons are
pampered, the mood is convivial yet decorous, and reservations are
honored (if you can get one - Bostonians are no dummies). Listed under
Italian, the food is better classifed as "European" since the chef/owner, a
star among stars, gives a French, maybe a Portuguese (and beyond) twist
to his cuisine; high-end of moderately priced.

Bennino's, 1234 Soldiers Field Rd, Brighton, 254-4336
7 a.m.-9 p.m Sun-Thurs, to 10 p.m. Fri & Sat
A convenient place to line the stomach in a most satisfying way before moving
on to the adjacent club and ballroom - sort of one-stop nightlife (see **CLUBS**
listings under **Cafe Grappa** and **Rivermore Ballroom**); family style at reasonable
prices; located in The Day's Inn, so ample parking is available and hopefully a
room if you forsake the dancing and drink more than you eat.

Uva, 1418 Commonwealth Ave, Brighton, 566-5670
5 p.m.-10 p.m. Mon-Thurs, to 11 Fri & Sat
Uva means grape, but wrath never makes the emotion list at this worth-

the-travel, not-to-be-missed restaurant; Pastaria offers four types of pasta noodles and a one-size, brick-oven hand-tossed pizza with four basic sauces, but you get to choose from some 30 fresh and fabulous ingredients to enhance them for 50 cents to $1.50 apiece; the Grill serves full dinners ($8-$15); unusual, yummy desserts; impressive, reasonably priced wine list.

Enzo's, 329 Harvard St, Brookline, 277-1288
11 a.m.-10:30 p.m. Mon-Sat, opens at 10 for brunch Sun; valet $3
So typical a trattoria, it's almost hokey, but it's hard to resist its charm, accented by the wandering violin/accordian duo; good food, good service and all-round pleasant experience for around $60 per couple; just beer and wine.

Kosher

Shalom Hunan, 92 Harvard St, Brookline, 731-9778
Parking in rear; 11:30 a.m.-10:30 p.m. Mon-Thurs, to 3 p.m. Fri, 6:30 p.m.-12 Sat, 12:30 p.m-10:30 Sun
Oy Vay, would you believe kosher Chinese food? Would we lie? It's given the seal of approval by the local kosher cops and has just about everything any other Chinese restaurant has except shell fish and, of course, the "P" word (pork), mainly subsituted by veal.

**Shang Chai Delight Vegetarian Restaurant, 404A Harvard St, Brookline, 232-2424
11 a.m.-9:30 p.m. Mon-Thurs & Sun; to 6 p.m. Fri, closed Sat; parking in rear
Chinese selections from column A and American from Column B; a vegetarian restaurant where the Oriental "steak" is made from soybean and other ingredients no self respecting cow would ever own up to, but the preparation of choice for self-respecting, non-flesh eaters.

Rubin's Kosher Delicatessen & Restaurant, 500 Harvard St, Brookline, 731-8787
10 a.m.-8 p.m. Sun-Thurs, to 3 p.m. Fri, closed Sat
A good place for a corned beef sandwich on rye with half sour pickles or other deli delights whether you require kosher or not, but don't ask for

real cream for your coffee or sour cream on your potato pancakes - no dairy here to mix in with the meat (God forbid!).

Victor's Pizza, 1364 Beacon St, Brookline 730-9903
11 a.m-8 p.m. weekdays
Pizza, pasta, salads, fish and chips that pass the scrutiny of a pious rabbi, in other words, strictly kosher; delivers anything locally but only large orders to Boston area; no spirits.

Russian

Yelena, 298 Washington St, Brighton, 787-0037
Open only on Sat & Sun 5 p.m-1 a.m., cash only
Definitely Moscow on the Charles (River); the borscht and shish kebab will make you want to dance the kazatsky (Russian folk dance); and dance you can to a live band, but contemporary music (no boot stomping); international crowd who generally dress up. Wine is offered but vodka dominates the spirits list (what else?) and can be purchased by the bottle if you really intend to go native. However, you are expected to enjoy it to the last drop since it's bad luck, say the Russians, not to finish the bottle once it has been opened. Aspirin anyone?

Seafood

Captain's Wharf, 356 Harvard St, Brookline, 566-5590
11 a.m.-10 p.m. Mon-Sat, 4 p.m.-9 Sun; CC for bill but cash only for gratuity
Reservations only for groups of 6 or more; free parking; beer and wine
Dock here for the freshest seafood and large portions at bargain prices (1-lb lobster or shrimp dinner specials are usually around $10). Even the service is good and the line (escapable only during off hours) goes quickly.

Tex/Mex

Armadillo Cafe, 1314 Comm. Ave, Allston, 232-4242
Noon-10 p.m. Sun, 5 p.m.-10 p.m. Mon-Wed, noon-10 p.m. Thurs, to 11 Fri & Sat (for food)

Food is Tex (barbecue, etc, $5-$14), and the ambience is Mex - roving mariachi bands Wed, guitarist/singer Fri & Sat; see **CLUBS** listing for late night entertainment.

CHINATOWN

Boston's Chinatown is the fourth largest in America. Its 30,000 residents maintain strong cultural ties to the Far East. Throughout the contained area, located just south of Downtown Crossing in the midst of Boston's financial, retail and theatre districts, one can see the tenacity to these Oriental traditions in the food, merchandise, festivities and activities. Shops display an array of Far Eastern delights including cloisonne, jade, porcelains, fabrics, clothing, groceries, herbs and spices, generally at reasonable prices. Ancestral remedies and treatments for a variety of maladies are also available. One can nicely and reasonably fend off a crab Rangoon attack at just about any of the myriad restaurants, many staying open until the wee hours of the morning. Most offer authentic Asian cuisine, satisfying Oriental tastes as well as catering to Occidentals who wield chopsticks as if to the Pagoda born. Here are some suggestions to guide you through the bamboo labyrinth. Street parking is rarely available, but there are garages and lots, and many restaurants validate.

Chinese

*Dynasty, 33 Edinboro Street, (near the dragon gateway) 350-7777
8 a.m.-4 a.m. daily
Almost as regal as its name with the help of a lot of brass and glass; a Hong Kong chef who brings his Hong Kong style of original dishes from the provinces of Cathay; abandon the pork fried rice mentality here and go for such delights as "Imperial Dungenese" (fresh soft-shelled crabs pan sauteed in their shell) or "Turnip Cake" (whole turnip chopped with shrimp and Chinese sausage steamed or pan fried); full bar service; entrees $10-$20.

*East Ocean City, 25-29 Beach Street, 542-2504
11 a.m.-3 a.m. Sun.-Thurs, to 4 a.m. Fri & Sat; validated parking after 5:30 p.m. $2
Among the best authentic seafood cuisines (Northern Chinese) at affordable prices; pick your own victim from the tanks that line the walls (referred to more elegantly by the owners as "crystalline aquariums").

*Chau Chow, 52 Beach St, 426-6266
10 a.m.-2 a.m. 7 days; no reservations or credit cards
You can do some great chow-chowing here fairly inexpensively if you don't mind cramped quarters; beer only.

*Grand Chau Chow, 41-45 Beach St, 292-5166
10:30 a.m.-2 a.m. Sun-Thurs, to 4 a.m. Fri & Sat
Accepts reservations and credit cards unlike its venerable ancestor, Chau Chow, across the street, and is three times the size; both considered by many of the discerning to be among the best in Chinatown; two can feast for about $30; just beer and wine.

*Moon Villa, 15 Edinboro St, 423-2061
11 a.m-4 a.m. 7 days; parking in rear after 6 p.m.
Another popular late-night hangout for the pre-hungover who are easily satisfied with the mundane Cantonese/Mandarin dishes for low prices; just beer.

*Ocean Wealth, 8 Tyler St., 423-1338
11 a.m-4 a.m. daily
The bounty of the Pacific Ocean such as eels, baby octopus and jelly fish, prepared in authentic Hong Kong style, is the specialty in this two-floored restaurant frequented by some of Boston's most famous chefs (suffice to say about the quality of the food), and the service is good, too— tuxedoed waiters living up to their satorial splendor; moderately priced for the moderate eater; beer and wine only; upper floor is a late-night hangout for the hip who aren't hipped out yet.

China Grove, formerly Taiwan Taste, 10 Tyler St, 542-5857
11:30 a.m.-10:30 p.m. weekdays, to 12:30 weekends
Same owner, different chef who, judging from the preponderance of Oriental patrons, appears to be as good, if not better, than the last one but with more variety - Peking and Szechuen in addition to Taiwanese; reservations suggested for weekends when the crowds really roll in.

People's Cafeteria, 21-23 Edinboro St., 482-7328
8 a.m.-10 p.m. Sun.-Thurs, to 10:30 Fri & Sat; cash only

Tucked away three stories up from street level, a no-frills gem for good Chinese food at attractive prices, ergo the name, contrary to its seemingly political connotations; features daily specials; beer and wine; self serve or wait person - the choice is yours.

Hong Kong Eatery, 79 Harrison Ave, 423-0838
9 a.m.-11 p.m. 7 days; cash only
Looks like a deli from the outside with the meats, etc. hanging from strings in the window; inside pleasant and bright with about 15 tables and comfortable cushioned seats; a nice variety of dishes, some unique, at reasonable prices; 35 versions of rice plates from $4.25-$5.50, each easily a meal in itself.

Eclectic Eastern

*Chinatown Eatery, 44 Beach St, Second Floor; cash only; no bar service 10:30 a.m.-1 or 2 a.m. depending on how busy; five restaurants (4 Chinese and 1 Thai) with their own cooking stalls sharing a common dining area. Emperor's Kitchen, 357-5430; Swatow, 423-6482; Wua Pei, 423-3685; Mak Kwan, 423-4593; Rod Thai, 357-9188
Ignore the lack of ambience (and that's a kind way of describing it) and concentrate on the array of succulent foods available at incredibly low prices. Wau Pei, for one, offers an astonishing variety of rice plates, 97, for $3.95-$4.50. Asians, mostly students, far outnumber the Occidentals, who have not yet discovered this place. As one of the restaurants boasts, you "eat like the emperor, pay like a student." I couldn't have said it better.

Vietnamese

Dong Khanh, 83 Harrison St., 426-9410
9:30 a.m.-11 p.m. daily; no credit cards; soft drinks only
The best Vietnamese food west of the Mekong Delta say a lot of doctors at neighboring Tufts Medical Center as well as Boston's Vietnamese population, who don't want anyone else to find out. The humble interior belies its culinary capacities - an amazing variety of rice, vegetables, noodles, meats and seafood, steamed or boiled (no greasy kid stuff here), blended and spiced to enhance natural flavors and preserve

nutritional value; all this at an average entree price of $5; try one of the more than 40 original, non-alcoholic drinks offered, predominately based in coffee, fruit juices and Ovaltine (bet you thought they didn't make that anymore).

Pho Pasteur, two Chinatown locations 8 Kneeland St, 451-0247; 682 Washington St, 482-7467
8 a.m.-8 p.m. Sun-Thurs, to 9 Fri & Sat; cash only
Great pho (soups) for very litte dough; see RESTAURANT listing under **Brighton.**

.****Buddha's Delight Vegetarian Restaurant,** 5 Beach St, 451-2395
11 a.m.-10 p.m. 7 days; cash only; no liquor
The non-kosher Vietnamese version of **Shang Chai Delight** (see BRIGHTON/ALLSTON/BROOKLINE listing under **Kosher**) under same ownership; reasonable prices ($4-$12).

DOWNTOWN

Boston's downtown area consists mainly of Washington Street, where retailing giants Filene's and Jordan Marsh are located, and the parallel Tremont Street with several perpendicular streets between the two, lined with myriad shops and boutiques. In the center of this area is Downtown Crossing, three or four city blocks converted into a pedestrian mall from which vehicular traffic is banned. Boston's jewlery center is also located here.

American

West Street Grill, 15 West St, 423-0300
5:30 p.m.-10 p.m. Mon & Tues, to 10:30 Wed-Sat, 11 a.m.-4 p.m. Sun;
Open for lunch; bar open to 2 a.m. Mon-Sat; reservations for six or more; parking next door, no validation
Young, mostly single Bostonians are taking Horace Greeley's advice to "Go West, young man" seriously, trekking in droves to this newest, trendy hot spot, so be prepared to wait; three floors (in a historic townhouse) of disparate dining and decor; African mahogany bar on the first floor, where the in-vogue wash down tasty appetizers with their martinis; romantic with soft lighting and banquettes here and on second level; third-floor dining room more formal and more expensive (dinner for two with wine about

$70); food, however, is secondary to the clientele who are there mainly to check out possible candidates for companionship for a lifetime, a night, or a couple of hours, and not necessarily in that order; live music (See **CLUBS** listings).

The Bay Tower Room, 60 State St, 723-1666
5:30 p.m-1 a.m. Mon-Thurs, to 2 a.m. Fri & Sat; validated garage parking
Just ten more steps or so and you cross the line to the Waterfront area, but the view of the city from this 33rd-floor aerie puts you in the middle of everywhere. And the food matches the fabulous view, not to mention the service, and I am; entrees from $15 to $27; "proper dress" requested; one of the few places in Boston where you can dance and dine at the same time - the cocktail lounge/piano bar is just above the dining room - a great interlude between courses. (See **CLUBS** listings for details on lounge.)

Dakota's, 34 Summer St, 737-1777
11:30 a.m.-10 p.m. Sun-Fri, opens 5:30 p.m. Sat
Validated parking in Lafayette Garage (next to Jordan Marsh)
Classy, mahogany-panelled, and marble-floored overlooking Downtown Crossing; mesquite-grilled seafood and steaks; a bit pricey (entrees $13-$30), but most of its patrons (many on expense accounts) don't have to worry about that.

The New Place, 14 Pie Alley (across from Devonshire St), 367-6430
8 a.m.-1 a.m. 7 days; discounted garage parking after 4 p.m.
Really an old place (21 years on Quaker Lane) but in a new location; pub food, cheap (served until 10 p.m) and pub atmosphere where young professionals mix and mingle and sometimes dance to the juke box when the crowd starts cookin' later in the evening.

The Last Hurrah Bar and Grill, Omni Parker House Hotel, 60 School St, 227-8600
11:30 a.m.-midnight Mon-Thurs, to 1 a.m. Fri & Sat; valet parking $22 (truly, not a typo)
First with local celebrities and politicians for a hearty (though uninspired), moderately priced ($12-$16), classic American meal with plenty of esprit de corps; located in Boston's oldest hotel, the birthplace of Parker House rolls; music and dancing starting at 7:30 Thurs-Sat.

BOSTON BY NIGHT

Continental

Locke-Ober, 3 Winter Pl, 542-1340
3 p.m.-10 p.m. daily for dinner; also serves lunch; valet after 6 p.m. $5
This is one of those places that must be mentioned in any book about
Boston - the sanctuary for Boston Brahmins since 1875 with a decor Queen
Victoria would approve of; the menu is extensive but uncreative and the
service impeccable but hardly warm; first-floor bar (for men only before it
went coed in the '70s) is more casual than the club-like, elegant second-
floor dining room with an a la carte menu that could result in a steep tab
(entrees $18-$39).

French

Maison Robert, 45 School St, 227-3370
5:30 p.m.-10 p.m. Mon-Fri, to 10:30 Sat; also serves lunch; valet parking $8.
Ooh la la, a Francophile's delight; fine classical French cuisine both in a
relaxed (the downstairs Ben's Cafe) or in a formal (the first-floor
Bonhomme Richard) setting; two prix fixe dinners at $15 or $22 in Cafe,
entrees $15-$30 in Bonhomme; located in Boston's former City Hall on the
Freedom Trail and a mini shrine to Benjamin Franklin; jackets and ties
required for the dining room; cafe features a French singer on Friday
nights; where the truly suave and sophisticated gather on a regular basis.

Tex/Mex

Fajitas & 'Ritas, 25 West St, 426-1222
11 a.m.-9 p.m. Mon-Wed, to 10 Thurs, to 11 Fri & Sat; reservations for 8 or more
Almost everything sizzles here - certainly the lively crowd and the fajitas -
except the margaritas, which are frosty and delicious; price range low-to-
moderate ($6-$10); also in Brookline.

FENWAY

A descriptive name for what this area used to be up to the eighteenth
century - a stretch of festering swamps and bogs. Reclaimed in the

nineteenth century as parkland called the Back Bay Fens, this sweeping section dominated by Fenway Park, the Museum of Fine Arts, Symphony Hall, Northeastern University and Harvard Medical School is principally populated by employees of or students at the many cultural, health and educational institutions located here. Traces of former residents, the Victorian gentry, still remain in the architecture of the buildings that survived the march of progress. An array of diverse restaurants, in price, formality and ethnicity, cater to the extensive range of tastes and needs of locals and visitors.

American

Boston Beer Works, 61 Brookline Ave, 536-Beer
11:30 a.m.-1 a.m daily; parking in lot next door, no validation
A beer-lovers Valhalla and fun for the non-imbiber as well; a working brewery visible from the restaurant/bar; rendezvous for Red Sox fans (Fenway Park is across the street) and other sports enthusiasts who like to mix pleasure with the business of watching sporting events (on a wide-screen TV); rib-sticking foods such as burgers and steaks; also appetizers; from $6-$14.

Cajun

Dixie Kitchen, 182 Mass. Ave, 526-3068
11:30 a.m.-11 p.m. Mon-Sat, 3 p.m-11 p.m. Sun
A real tongue burner for under $10; authentic Creole with all the trappings—madi gras motiff; 60 seats; lots of spirit but no spirits.

Japanese

Goeman Japanese Noodle, 267 Huntington Ave, 859-8669
11:30 a.m.-10 p.m. Sun-Thurs, to 11 Fri & Sat; reservations for more than 6
The Japanese were eating noodles centuries before the Italians ever heard of them, and all that history is put to best advantage at this popular noodle house; pick your shape and size from the noodle display, then from a long list of ingredients, all of which end up in a steamy, delicious broth fit for the emperor; also tasty appetizers and tempura, all for $3 to $9; just beer and wine.

Mexican

Sol Azteca, 914A Beacon St, 262-0909
5 p.m.-10:30 p.m. Mon-Thurs, to 11 Fri & Sat, to 10 Sun
Since I won't even stand in the same room with red hot chile peppers
unless it's the band with the same name, you'll have to take the word of
those who do and Boston Magazine, which rated this "best" in one of its
annual "Best and Worst" issues; moderately priced; frequented by those
who do like it hot and that's more than some.

Middle Eastern

*Sami's, 299 Longwood Ave (across from Children's Hospital), 232-7175
24 hours daily
A Middle Eastern, pullman-car-shaped diner that also serves some
Mexican appetizers and deli sandwiches, all at bargain prices; caters to
hospital employees and visitors by day and to the party crowd late night.

Thai

Bangkok Cuisine, 177 Mass. Ave, 262-5377
11:30 a.m.-10:30 p.m. Mon-Thurs, to 11 Fri & Sat, 4 p.m.-10 p.m. Sun
One of the first Thai restaurants in Boston and still one of the best; main
dishes range from $8-$10; the duck with cashew nuts and other exotic
flavors is one of its best bets; just beer and wine.

FINANCIAL DISTRICT/SOUTH STATION

Boston's equivalent to New York's Wall Street, the Financial District is made
up of one square mile of fairly new or refurbished highrise buildings
housing the headquarters for investment and banking institutions. Restaurants and bars here generally cater to an after-work crowd, closing
around 8:30 or 9 p.m. on week nights and on weekends when their
clientele clears out to turn their attention to other dividends. Some newer,
more visionary entrepreneurial types, however, are expanding their
target markets hoping to make the Financial District as hot by night as by

day but with a more hedonistic bent. Thusfar, they have one significant advantage of abundant street parking on weekends when all business is shut tight. On the southern fringe of the district is South Station, where waiting for buses and trains is almost a pleasure in this beautifully refurbished, smoke-free transportation center offering an impressive assortment of tempting foods, goods, and services. Since several art galleries operate in the area surrounding South Station, many restaurants and bars here showcase the works of aspiring artists who make up a large segment of their following.

American

The Art Zone, 150 Kneeland St, 695-0087
11:30 a.m.-9:30 p.m. Mon-Fri, 5-8:30 Sat, 11:30-8:30 Sun
"Industrial" is the best word to describe the cement-floored, exposed-lighting decor relieved by art exhibits featuring a new artist each month (even the tables are dioramas under glass); one of the best places in town for Texas barbecue—ribs, chicken and fish prepared on wood-fueled, open flame; great beer selection; favored by bankers as well as hardhats and the "artsy" set.

*Blue Diner, 158 Kneeland St, 338-4639
24 hours Tues-Sat
A '50s diner whose main appeal is the large portions of reasonably priced "home-cooked" food and that it's there all the time (except Christmas Day) to serve the anxious who go to work at the crack of dawn, the construction workers who forgot their lunch pails, the swing shifters coming off night duty, and the tuxedoed bon vivant coming off night duty; owned by the same gentlemen who brings us The Art Zone.

Goodfella's, 105 Water St,, 338-2233
11:30 a.m.-9p.m. Mon-Wed, to 10:30 or 11 Thurs. & Fri; no reservations
Contrary to its name, nary a suspicious character in sight; the narrow space where the long bar is located makes for good eavesdropping on what's happening in the stock market, the general topic of conversation for the financial types who go there; basic American fare with an Italian twist; medium to low price range; well lit and attractively decorated.

Brandy Pete's, 267 Franklin St., 439-4165
11:30 a.m.-10 p.m. Mon-Fri; bar open to midnight
Most notable foodwise for its selection of hard-to-find old Boston dishes, satisfying if you're not too fussy and reasonably priced. The real attraction here is the bar where men, financial types, do a lot of bonding, hardly noticing the occasional, attractive females who dare to storm their bastion. Lobby bar features a pianist from 5 p.m. to 8 p.m.

Australian

Ayers Rock, 112 Broad St, 542-2021
11:30 a.m-1 a.m (food served until 10 p.m.)
No billabongs to cross to reach this outback; upscaled pub food Aussie style and very reasonably priced even by American standards; Crocodile Dundee would feel at ease in this rustic, aborigine-inspired setting; features large selection of Australian wines and beers.

Continental

Julien, 250 Franklin St, 451-1900
6 p.m.-9:45 p.m. daily; also serves lunch; free valet or garage parking
In the Hotel Meridien, once the Federal Reserve building; elegance at its most elegant; flawless menu, flawless service; expensive but an experience to remember; worthy to carry the name of Boston's first French restaurant located on that site (or nearabouts) in the late 18th century.

International

*The Eatery, 44 Batterymarch St, 426-2969
5 p.m.-5 a.m. Mon-Sat; no credit cards
New to the scene (October, '93); sort of a fast-food diner but healthier—Middle Eastern, Italian and American selections with the accent on turkey dinners and a salad bar with nearly 60 items, all for $3-$7.

Italian

Il Panino, 295 Franklin St., 338-1000
Valet parking $7
Bistro, 5 p.m. - midnight Mon-Sat, open for lunch; no reservations accepted, but hot pizza to take the edge off while you wait for your table
Main dining room, 5:30 p.m.-10:30 p.m. Mon-Sat; must have reservations
Five floors of food (Tuscany Italian), fun and frolic sanctioned by the au courant; Bistro—casual dining at moderate cost ($11 and under); main dining room—a la carte, pricey menu, around $70 for two (a bit less if you drink only water) but twice that if you're into three courses and fine wines. That's the food! For the fun and frolic, cruise the top three floors (see **CLUBS** listings for description).

Japanese

Sakura-bana, 57 Broad St, 542-4311
5 p.m.-10 p.m Sun-Thurs, to 11 Fri & Sat
Popular, neighborhood low-frills, low-cost sushi bar, also tempura and teriaki; just beer, wine and, of course, saki.

Spanish

Cecil's, 129 South St, 542-5108
11:30 a.m.-10 p.m Mon-Fri, 5-10 p.m. Sat
A Cuban/Mexican cantina disguised as a New York "SoHo"-style restaurant where local artists hang out; good inexpensive, food and you can leave home without your American Express·card - they take everything but; live folk/jazz music on Saturday nights.

JAMAICA PLAIN

Once a blue-collar community, "JP," as alluded to by savvy locals, has been gentrified by artists, students and young professionals over the last decade or two. In not-so-beautiful downtown JP (but slowly rejuvinating), several upscale restaurants are operating at downscale prices along with coffee houses and cafes, all very worthwhile of a "T" ride on the Orange Line or 15-20 minutes by car.

American

*Doyle's Cafe, 3484 Washington St, 524-2345
9 a.m.-1 a.m. Mon-Sat, food to 11:30, pizza to closing
Free parking in rear; only cash or checks
A JP institution once a hangout for locals and pols, still displaying original signs such as "ham steak with mashed potatoes and peas for 45 cents;" now revitalized by the influx of yuppies and Generation X-ers from all over Greater Boston; mainly pub food from $2.50-$10.

International

Centre Street Cafe, 597 Centre St. (near corner of Pond St), 524-9217
5 p.m.-10 p.m. 7 nights, open for brunch (9 a.m.-3 p.m.) Wed-Sun
Reservations for 5 or more; cash or checks only
A funky 19-seat storefront that showcases a new, starving artist monthly, operated by a young, energetic woman who cooked her way through France for two years and returned home with a bagful of culinary secrets. Overused though the word may be, eclectic is the only way to describe the range of 15-or-so cultures she touches on to produce her freshest-of-the-fresh, cooked-to-order, mouth-watering dishes—six entrees on the standard menu ($6-$7) along with five specials each evening (a little higher priced since she uses more expensive ingredients as wild mush-rooms and smoked salmon). Most dishes start as basic vegetarian to which can be added chicken, shrimp or tofu. In answer to the question of "Where's the beef?" there is none, not in the food and certainly not with the quality, presentation or the prices. No liquor, but fresh-squeezed juices.

Black Crow Caffe, 2 Perkins St (off Centre St), 983-9231
9 a.m.-10 p.m. Mon-Sat, to 9 Sun
Reinforcing that funk is the "F" word of choice in JP, this 11-table storefront is also making ripples way beyond the area's boundary lines offering "gourmet" pastas, fresh fish and more for $7-$15; live jazz Mondays and Tuesdays from 6 p.m. to closing.

Coffee Contata Bistro and Beans, 605 Centre St, 522-2223
7:30 a.m-7 p.m. Mon-Wed, to 9 Thurs & Fri, to 10 Sat, 9-3 Sun; cash only

If the aroma of the fresh-roasted, select coffee beans doesn't drag you in, then the handmade raviolis and pastas (with light sauces), zucchini gondolas, fritatas or the delectable, baked-on-premise pastries certainly should; also 19 seats (seems to be a magic number in JP); no liquor but a full coffee bar menu; a high-energy meeting place for the artistic and educated.

Mexican

Tacos El Charro, 349 Centre St, 983-9275
9:30 a.m.-11:30 p.m. Mon-Thurs, to midnight Fri-Sun; just beer and wine
Adds more than a little spice to life with its traditional Mexican food (hot, hot, hot, $5-$12) and roving mariachi bands 7-11 p.m. Fri & Sat, 5-10 p.m. Sun, and 7-10 p.m. Mon; $1 cover charge Fri-Mon for non-eaters.

NORTH END

The oldest of Boston's residential neighborhoods, the North End is Italian to its core and has been since the 1920s. Its password is "Mangia!" (Eat!). This 100 acres just a hop and a skip from Faneuil Hall Marketplace boasts a concentration of Italian restaurants, cafes and bakeries unrivaled on this continent. Pick a place, any place, to eat, and you can't go wrong. And in true Italian fashion, finish up with an expresso or capuccino and a decadent pastry, maybe a little touch of Sambuca, at one of the many cafes or eat-in bakeries. Burn up some of the calories by taking a walk and capture a glimpse of the traditions that make this section so unique. Alas, this distinction is dissipating with the demise of those who cling to those traditions but whose progeny have left the old ways and the old neighborhood behind.

For those who prefer not to play the guessing game, here are some suggestions. Keep in mind that all roads lead to Hanover Street, the area's main drag. Street parking is practically non-existent, but there are garages on the perimeter of the area where parking fees range from $1 (for two hours) to $6 (for the evening).

Italian

Dolce Vita, 237 Hanover St, 720-0422
11 a.m.-11 p.m.; validated garage parking $1 for 2 hours
Food like your mama used to make if she happened to be Italian. Ask what's brewing in the kitchen since some of the best dishes are not listed on the menu; surprises dictated by what fresh and wonderful ingredients may be available on a given day; entrees $10-$18; quaint Italian setting; no dress code but guests typically gussie up; live accordianists or guitarists on some weekends; downstairs cafe open to 11:30 p.m.

Daily Catch, 323 Hanover St, 523-8567
11:30 a.m.-11 p.m. Mon-Sat, noon-11 Sun, no reservations; cash only
Really fresh seafood with a Sicilian twist; entrees $11.50-$16.50; tiny (20 seats) and cheery; just beer and wine.

Il Panino, 11 Parmenter St, 720-1336
11 a.m.-10 p.m. Sun-Thurs, to 11 Fri & Sat; no reservations; cash only
Don't let the pizza parlor/sub shop on the street level fool you—downstairs is a 40-seat classic trattoria where Italians from Italy dine while in Boston (need we say more?); no menu; waiters ask "how hungry are you?" and "what do you feel like eating tonight?"—if it's Italian, you'll get it; medium price range.

Pomodoro, 319 Hanover St, 367-4348
11 a.m.-11 p.m. daily
Considered by the newer, hipper residents of the North End to be the best in the neighborhood, "maybe the whole country;" regional Italian menu changes daily, sometimes including such exotic treats as wild boar or venison; occasional guest chefs provide even more variety; entrees range from $10-$20; just beer and wine; rotating art on the wall all for sale; still relatively undiscovered, yet patience is a must since there are only 12 tables.

Lo Conte's, 116 Salem St, 720-3550
11 a.m.-10:30 p.m Mon-Thurs, to 11 Fri & Sat; no reservations Fri & Sat
Validated parking $3 for 4 hours after 3 p.m.

Classic Italian food; huge portions (go for dinner and get enough for lunch the following day, too); very reasonably priced and they don't make up for it on their wines—they're low-cost, too, but nice for the price; the butcher-block tables with green inlays (to match the walls) and modern decor deviate from the traditional, white- or checkered-tableclothed motif.

Alloro, 351 Hanover St, 523-9268
5:30 p.m.-10 p.m. Mon-Thurs, to 10:30 Fri & Sat, 3-9 p.m. Sun; no credit cards
Mum's the word among its avid fans, mostly neighborhood folks and restaurant professionals, who want to keep to themselves this small (30 seats), inexpensive restaurant serving great Southern Italian food with Portuguese influence; a world wine list—at least two selections from just about anywhere for rarely more than $22 a bottle.

Davide, 326 Commercial St, 227-5745
5 p.m.-11 p.m. daily; valet parking $6; no sneakers or jeans
Lots of Old World charm; somewhat limited menu (for a North End restaurant) but offers enough diversity to please most and expertly prepared; service is friendly and professional. Ask for one of the wrap-around booths if you plan on proposing - romantic Davide is known as "the restaurant to get engaged in."

Terramia, 98 Salem St, 523-3112
5 p.m.-10 p.m. Mon-Thurs, to 11 Fri & Sat; also serves lunch
No reservations on weekends
The classic Coke of the North End - the real thing; Italian food at its most authentic say its devoted, discerning, impressive number of fans; Northern Italian with Southern influences; small - 40 seats; price range high end of moderate; superb wine list, mainly Italian, reasonably priced; frequented by neighborhood people and visitors from Italy yearning for a home-cooked meal as they know it.

Al Dente, 109 Salem St, 523-0990
11 a.m.-11 p.m. Mon-Sun; validated parking at nearby garage ($1 for 2 hrs.)
A Johnny-come-lately to the North End scene but already scooping out its niche in an overcrowded market mainly due to the distinguished reputation of its chef and his efforts not to rest on those laurels; varied menu

offers authentic Italian cuisine from all regions of Italy; relatively inexpensive - two can dine on appetizer and entree with wine for about $40.

Carlo Marino's, 8 Prince St, 523-9109
5 p.m.-10:30 p.m. Tues-Sat, validated parking $1 for 2 hours; no reservations on Sat
You can rely on good, basic, and traditional food here for moderate prices, which is why its patrons come back regularly; the owner's warm, inviting personality is another reason.

Giacomo's, 355 Hanover St, 523-9026
5:30 p.m.-10 p.m. Sun-Thurs, to 10:30 Fri & Sat; only American Express or cash
Traditional Italian to its checkered tablecloths; busy and crowded but worth the wait for both the quality and price (low moderate); second location in South End (see **SOUTH END** listing).

La Famiglia Giorgio's, 112 Salem St, 367-6711
4 p.m.-11 p.m. daily; parking in Allright garage $1 for 2 hrs.; no reservations
So successful, the family quickly branched out. (see description under **BACK BAY, Italian RESTAURANT listing)**

Cozy Corner, 162 Salem St, 523-7660
6:30 a.m.-8 p.m. Mon-Sat
The North End's version of a diner; no frills, no candlelight short of a power failure, but great homemade food cheap; no reservations, no parking and no credit cards, but no kidding, no one beats its pasta frigiole, a rib-sticker costing under $3.

Corner Cafe, 87 Prince St., 523-8997
8 a.m.-2 a.m. daily
One of the North End's favorite watering holes to watch sports, play pinball and munch on great Texas barbecue (with a side order of pasta?); lots of local color; full food service to 8 p.m., appetizers to 11.

Cafes and Eat-In Bakeries

Grand Cafe, 107 Salem St., 722-9383
9 a.m.-midnight daily

Desserts worth getting fat for; beautiful decor - marble floors and wood paneled; coffees and full liquor service.

Cafe Graffiti, 307 Hanover St., 367-3016
6 a.m.-midnight Mon-Sat; opens at 8 a.m. on Sunday
Homemade Italian pastries, coffees, full liquor license; great after-dinner meeting place to rub connolis with the locals; leave your mark on the North End by signing the wall - they don't call it Cafe Graffiti for nothing.

Caffe Vittoria, 296 Hanover St, 227-7606
8 a.m-midnight daily
Four floors, one smoke free, of Italian indulgence such as gelati and cannolis to name my favorites, savored with cappuccino or expresso; full liquor service.

*Bova's Bakery, 134 Salem St (corner of Prince St), 523-5601
Open 24 hours every day
Insominia City!-busy all night with those coming off or going on work or play; homemade Italian pastries that should be banned in Boston on the basis of their calorie and fat content, could tempt even Richard Simmons off his thin foods wagon. The coffees are great too.

Dolce Vita, 237 Hanover St., downstairs from the restaurant; 720-0422
11 a.m-11:30 p.m. daily
What's a good Italian dinner without dessert? -the sweet life at its sweetest and for only $1.50-$3.50; beer and wine.

NORTH STATION

The best-known edifice in this area wedged in between the North End and the waterfront is Boston Garden, home to the 16-time World-Champion Boston Celtics and five-time Stanley Cup Champion Boston Bruins as well as the site for the city's largest rock concerts, ice shows and circuses. Opened in 1928, this grand old lady with the famous parquet floor will be demolished when the new, adjacent arena, named Shawmut Center, is completed in the fall of 1995. Eateries and bars in this area have traditionally adjusted their menus, hours and entertainment according to what's happening at the Garden (ie, upscale for Celtics games, earthy for Bruins

BOSTON BY NIGHT

games and youth oriented for concerts). While many still do, new and refurbished clubs and pubs are now drawing crowds even when the Garden is dark (see CLUBS listings under NORTH STATION).

American

Commonwealth Brewing Co., 138 Portland St, 523-8383
11:30 a.m.-midnight Mon-Thurs, to 1 a.m. Fri & Sat, noon-10 p.m. Sun
Massachusetts' oldest, continuously operating brewery where copper is king (tabletops, bar, brewing kettles and other less obvious accessories); bold, big and casual atmosphere with food to match; free tours of the brewery but no sampling; music Fri & Sat (see CLUBS listing under NORTH STATION).

Bullfinch Barbeque, 141 Portland St, 523-8640
10:30 a.m.-2 a.m. daily (closes earlier if not busy)
Known for its "home-cooked" meatloaf and soups made from scratch in addition to usual barbeque selections $3-$9; entertainment and dancing (see CLUBS listings under NORTH STATION).

Asian

Celebrities, 262 Friend St, 723-2288
11:30 a.m.-10:30 p.m. 7 days
On the second floor of this three-story establishment, called the See-Da Thai Room, See-Da meaning "beautiful lady," according to the owner, and it is; spacious (110 seats); Thai and Korean specialties $5-$10; sports bar on the first floor, Ambassador Club on the third floor (see CLUBS listings under NORTH STATION).

Italian

Joe Tecce's Ristorante, 61 North Washington St, 742-6210
11:30 a.m.-11 p.m. 7 days; validated parking $8
Undistinguished, "red-sauce" type food (still loved by many) at $9-$18 for entrees, but the garish decor is draw enough if only as a curiousity factor;

34

seek out Joe himself, who is only too happy to give anyone who will listen the history behind all of his treasures.

Roma Rosticceria, 252 Friend St, 720-5037
Noon-11 p.m. 7 days; cash only
You'll stand on line for this tiny Italian diner (really a trailer) but it will be worth the wait—fresh and tasty, authentic cooking and hand-tossed pizza cheap.

SOUTH END

The term "gentrification" is synonomous with Boston's South End, one of the most distinctive of Boston's neighborhoods. Throughout the area, once-lavish, five-story townhouses that deteriorated when Boston's Brahmins abandoned the district for greener pastures, have been converted to multi-housing dwellings, attracting a multi-cultural, multi-ethnic, economically diverse blend of residents. Close on their heels came the shops, restaurants and cafes that reflect the flavor of the community.

American

St. Cloud, 557 Tremont St, 563-0202
5:30 p.m.-midnight daily, bar to 1 a.m, open for lunch; valet parking $7
More chi chi and larger than most of the local competition; good American/French cuisine $8-$23; both restaurant and bar favored by the well-dressed and the cosmopolitan.

Geoffrey's Cafe Bar, 578 Tremont St, 266-1122
8 a.m-10 p.m. Mon-Thurs, to 11 Sat & Sun; no reservations
You will see red here, but only when staring at the walls—no one could ever get upset with this dandy dining establishment serving great specialty sandwiches, pasta and other bistro fare in abundant portions ($7-$13) as well as yummy drinks and desserts; casual, amiable atmosphere (if you have nothing against red walls). Also on 651 Boylston St, Back Bay, 437-6400.

Blue Wave, 142 Berkeley St, 424-6664
11:30 a.m.-11 p.m. Mon-Fri, 5 p.m.-11:30 Sat, 10:30 a.m.-11 p.m. Sun
Valet parking Thurs-Sat $8; Boston's only truly dedicated exponent of

California cuisine--healthy, innovative and attractively presented (also an accurate description of its clientele); equally creative is the stylish West Coast decor; entrees begin at about the ticket price for a first-run movie $8.

Icarus, 3 Appleton St, 426-1790
6 p.m.-10 p.m Mon-Thurs, to 11 Fri, 5:30-11 Sat, 5:30-10 Sun; valet parking $8
Named after the mythical boy whose wings were clipped (actually melted) when he flew too close to the sun, Icarus, the restaurant, has also been flying high but basking in its place in the sun and deservedly so. Its succulent, seasonally changing, New American entrees don't come cheap—$17.50-$24; live jazz (piano and bass) Friday 7:30-11:30.

On The Park, 1 Union Park (at the corner of Shawmut Ave), 426-0862
5:30 p.m.-10:30 p.m. Mon-Thurs, to 11 Fri & Sat, to 9:30 Sun; reservations for 6 or more
Providing creative, tempting food and good service is a walk in the park for this small, intimate eatery consistently drawing the A-crowd; entrees range from $6-$16.

Claddagh, 335 Columbus Ave, 262-9874
11 a.m.-1 a.m. daily; garage parking across the street $7
Not your typical Irish pub even though it's named after a place in Galway; prefers to be considered a "Euro bistro;" some Irish dishes as part of its "American/European cuisine;" recently remodeled and expanded, in both structure and attitude, looking for a larger share of the upscale market that is finding the South End so fascinating; moderately priced and rising; live music (Irish, R&B and contemporary) and dancing Wed, Fri & Sat.

Asian

Jae's Cafe and Grill, 520 Columbus Ave, 421-9405
11:30 a.m.-10:30 p.m.; valet parking $7; reservations for 6 or more
Actually pan-Asian with Korean and Thai influences, also Sushi; several selections from the heart of Seoul but ask for a pitcher of water before digging in to be ready to douse the fire; decor is a blast from the past with wild, psychedelic, splash-painted walls but Jae's is not just for flower children - for anyone looking for excellent food at reasonable prices.

Continental

St. Botolph, 99 St. Botolph St, 266-3030
11:30 a.m-midnight daily; valet parking Tues-Sat $8
Located in a typical, South End bi-level brownstone with all the charm;
gourmet pizzas and then some in the cafe ($6-$12); dinner with Italian flair
(consistently good) from $14-$24; informal elegance; considered by South
Enders to serve the best martinis in the area.

Ethiopean

Addis Red Sea, 544 Tremont St, 426-8727
5 p.m.-11 p.m. Mon-Fri, noon-midnight Sat & Sun
A glimpse of Ethiopia without the 14-hour plane ride right down to the
mesobs (low-rattan tables), chairs about half the height of customary
seats, colorful native rugs and wall hangings, and background music;
servers wear traditional dress to add to the scenario; authentic Ethiopean
cuisine—mostly spicey but mild dishes are available on request; all this
atmosphere and charm, yet low end of moderate prices.

French

Hammersley's, 553 Tremont St, 423-2700
6 p.m.-10 p.m Mon-Thurs, to 10:30 Fri & Sat, to 9:30 Sun; valet Parking $8
Undoubtedly the reigning queen of the South End and a good candi-
date for royalty in any neighborhood; soft yellow walls (with black ac-
cents) stay cleaner, longer in this smoke-free restaurant; entrees range
from $16.50-$28; $16.50-pp food minimum.

International

Claremont Cafe, 535 Columbus Ave, 247-9001
7:30 a.m.-10 p.m. Mon-Thurs, to 10:30 Sat, 9 a.m.-3 p.m. Sun
Cash/checks; no reservations
A neighborhood gem any neighborhood would be proud to claim; the
South American chef keeps on delighting (and often surprising) his patrons
with his world cuisine; small (15 tables) but spilling out to the sidewalk in
pleasant weather; reasonably priced.

Bluestone Bistro, 480A Columbus Ave, 536-9331
5 p.m.-11 p.m. Sun-Thurs, to 12 Fri & Sat; no reservations
Talk about your neighborhood gem—this one absolutely sparkles; a
square of blue stone in the center of each table reminds patrons where
they are dining, but few will forget this cozy (48 seats), contemporary
bistro where the food is fresh and creative and the prices are moderate;
just wine and beer.

Italian

Azita Ristorante, 560 Tremont St, 338-8070
5:30 p.m.-10 p.m. Mon-Thurs, to 11 Fri & Sat; open for lunch
Valet parking $7 or in Berkeley St. garage $5
Romeo and Juliet would gladly have traded the balcony for this place—
it's romantic, intimate and pretty in pink (with white and black); atrium
seating in the rear; Northern Italian cuisine - inventive pasta dishes $9-$13,
imaginative meat/poultry/seafood entrees $15-$19; an unusual selection of
California wines.

botolph's on Tremont, 569 Tremont St, 424-8577
11:30 a.m.-11:30 p.m. daily; reservations for 8 or more
Would you believe Italian with an Asian twist? Well, pasta did originate in
the Orient! An open, airy, lively cafe, crisp in black, red and white; larger
than most of the other South End eateries but still in the same ball park
price wise ($4.50-$16.50).

*Anchovie's, 433 Columbus Ave, 266-5088
4 p.m.-2 a.m. Mon-Sat; no reservations
A cross between a pub and a trattoria; hearty, fresh, tasty food in generous portions and inexpensive ($5-$10); the bar, which takes up half of its
limited space, is always lively with locals.

Giacomo's, 431 Columbus Ave, 536-5723
5 p.m.-10 p.m. Mon-Thurs to 11 Fri-Sun; valet $8
Opened in Spring of '94, it is banking on its good reputation from its
North End restaurant (see **NORTH END** listing) to succeed here and
undoubtedly will if they deliver the same quality. Deviating from the

traditional decor of the original, this one is more contemporary with an open kitchen and a mosaic ceiling; 50 seats; entrees from $10-$16; mainly seafood; just beer and wine.

Appetito, 1 Appleton St, 338-6777
5 p.m.-10 p.m. Sun-Thurs, to 11 Fri & Sat; valet parking $4
Highly successful in Newton, Appetito has recently come (spring, '94) to the South End with its light Northern Italian cuisine for $5-$19 and a separate bar to wait in comfort, which is predetermined if we use the Newton branch as our gauge.

Latin American

Botucatu, 57 W. Dedham St, 247-9249
11:30 a.m.-10 p.m. Mon-Thurs, to 11 Fri & Sat, 3-10 p.m. Sun; parking in rear in post office lot (after 5 p.m.)
Three different chefs putting their own geographic touch in the creation of the good Mexican/Brazilian/Spanish cuisine offered here at reasonable prices in a friendly, family atmosphere; just beer and wine and, of course, lots of water.

Southern

Bob the Chef, 604 Columbus Ave, 536-6204
8 a.m.-9 p.m. Sun-Thurs, to 11 Fri & Sat
Real Southern, down-home, soul cooking complete with collard greens, ham hocks, ribs, black-eyed peas and fluffy biscuits; better than reasonably priced, downright inexpensive; funky, full of neighborhood charm, and plenty of Southern hospitality to yo' all; just wine and beer.

THEATRE DISTRICT

Boston's four large, legitimate theatres are clustered in one area, three on Tremont St and one around the corner on Boylston, and have long been the venues for pre-Broadway tryouts of new productions and a popular stop for touring shows. Several other smaller theatres also flourish. Restaurants here cater to pre-theatre goers who dine with one eye on the clock.

BOSTON BY NIGHT

American

*Remington's of Boston, 124 Boylston St., 574-9676
11 a.m.-2 a.m. daily; food served until 1:30 a.m. Thurs-Sat
A converted bank but the deposits are now made for the reasonably
priced food with the interest on the long list of beers, wines and specialty
drinks; could be your only chance to sit in a vault - the downstairs dining
area; big before-and-after theatre crowd and a late-night hangout for
bartenders coming off earlier shifts.

Chinese

Joyce Chen, 115 Stuart St, 720-1331
11:30 a.m.-10 p.m. Mon-Thurs & Sun, to midnight Fri & Sat
Parking lot across the street - no validation; reservations for 5 or more
The legacy of Joyce Chen, cookbook author and TV personality, is carried
on by her son who offers Szechuan, Mandarin and Shanghai dishes, truly
as mother used to make them, at very reasonable prices; separate
lounge offers same menu or a quick bite.

German

Jacob Wirth, 31-37 Stuart St, 338-8586
Noon-8 p.m. Sun, 11:30 a.m.-8 p.m. Mon, to 11:30 Tues-Thurs, to midnight Fri &
Sat; validated parking next door, free for first hour
Boston's only German restaurant and the city's third oldest (126 years), they
must be doing something right; noted for its knockwurst, brockwurst and other
German goodies but also offers such American classics as prime rib; entrees from
$9-$14; fashioned after a German beer hall complete with sawdust on the floor;
known as "Boston's best beer bar," featuring its own special dark brew along
with a host of others; sing-a-long on Fridays 8 p.m-midnight.

Greek

Omonia, 75 S. Charles St, 426-4310
11:30 a.m.-10 p.m. Tues-Sat, noon-9 p.m. Sun
Validated garage parking next door, $3

You'll have to resist the urge to toss the dishes here, it's so reminiscent of a taverna on a Greek Island where platter demolition is not only allowed but encouraged (and added to the bill), particularly when the ouzo takes control; classic, well-prepared Greek dishes such as shish kebab, souvlaki and moussaka (save room for the baklava); good selection of Greek wines among others; Greek background music completes the Aegean experience.

Italian

Galleria Italiana, 177 Tremont St (near Boylston), 423-2092
7 a.m.-10 p.m. Mon-Fri (closed 5-5:30), 5:30-10 p.m. Sat
Its locale may not be a treat for the eyes but that fades into the realm of "Who cares!" when compared to the creative Abruzzi-based fare, the charming presentation, nice service and easy-on-the-pocket prices (entrees $8-$14). Serving only breakfast and lunch up to Jan '94, it has found its real niche in dinner. Bostonians have yet to find that out, but that discovery is only a few words of mouths and/or a glowing review away.

International

Marais, 116 Boylston St, 482-7799
5:30-10 p.m. Mon-Wed, to 11 Thurs-Sat, bar open 4:30-2 a.m. Mon-Sat
Boasts the longest bar in town and rarely a vacant stool; tables line the opposite wall (the Bistro) for diners who like to be part of the bar action (plenty of that); also a separate, quieter dining room; French/Mediterranean cuisine (moderately priced); a meeting place for all ages and stages; Nightclub in rear (see **CLUB** listings in **THEATRE DISTRICT** section under **Esmé**).

David's, 123 Stuart St, (in the Transportation Building) 367-8405
11:30 a.m.-11:30 p.m. Tues-Fri, 5-11:30 Sat, 4-9 Sun
Cuisine is like a marauding army marching from France to Italy, onto North Africa and Greece; recently expanded to accommodate a growing (well dressed) clientele who enjoy the variety (and the large portions) at moderate prices (entrees $13-$21).

Vietnamese

Pho Bolsa, 1 Stuart St, 695-1843
10 a.m-midnight daily
The accent is on health here which could be why there are no evil spirits
(alcholic beverages). Loosely translated, "pho" means a bowl of light
broth poured over chicken or beef with rice noodles; you pick the varia-
tions. Health comes fairly cheap here - entrees from $4-$12.50.

WATERFRONT

Boston has one of the most exciting waterfronts in the world and it all
began with the reopening of Quincy Market in 1975. This was history
repeating itself in the most positive way. The original Quincy Market was
opened in 1826 as Boston's first food market and operated until the
1950s. The restored Quincy Market, renamed Faneuil Hall Market Place
and consisting of restaurants and shops, was an instant success, leading to
two major expansions. The South Market Building opened in 1977 and
the North Market Building in 1978. The complex is now among the most
popular attractions in the country, drawing some 15 million visitors annually.
Not even a visitor from the wilds of Borneo needs a definitive guide
through the Market. One could shoot an arrow in any direction and hit a
restaurant or cafe where the food is good, generally reasonably priced,
and well situated for people watching. If you don't mind dining "a la
pied" (standing up), the Food Court offers a cornucopia of native and
international foods. One leisurely stroll from beginning to end could result
in a three-pound weight gain from the aromas alone. We would be
remiss in not pointing out the one must-visit restaurant in the Market,
Durgin- Park, where little has changed since the Colonials sipped and
supped there. See **RESTAURANTS** Listing for particulars. Just beyond the
Market, other eating and drinking establishments dot the wharves from
Commercial Street to Northern Avenue (the fish pier) and are well worth
the walk.

Japanese

Tatsukichi, 189 State St, 720-2468
5 p.m.-10 p.m. Mon-Wed, to 11 Thurs-Sat, to 9:30 Sun
A Japanese restaurant for the Japanese and all others who love fresh, consistently good, authentic Japanese food ($2.50-$22); Karaoke 7 p.m.-1 a.m. nightly.

Seafood

Durgin-Park, Faneuil Hall, 227-2038
11:30 a.m.-10 p.m. daily; reservations for 5 or more weekdays, none on weekends
A Boston landmark changed little since our great-great-grandfathers dined there; typical colonial-inn decor; known for its less-than-polite service but the seafood is fresh and portions plentiful ($6-$30); music nightly in the Oyster Bar where appetizers are available until closing.

Union Oyster House, 41 Union St, 227-2750
11 a.m-9:30 p.m. (late supper to 11) Sun-Thurs, to 10
(Late supper to Midnight) Fri & Sat
America's oldest restaurant (since 1826 in a building over 250 years old); another landmark that shouldn't be missed but more for the historic value than the food; first-floor oyster bar (unchanged since Daniel Webster started everyday there with six tumblers of brandy and three dozen oysters); restaurant above featuring, what else?, seafood; moderately priced; locals stick with the oyster bar while the restaurant is filled with tourists who have to try it at least once.

Four Winds Seafood Grille, 266 Commercial St, 742-3922
Noon to 2 a.m. (food to 10 or 11) seven days; nearby parking lots
Known affectionately as "a Big Living Room" to the regulars who are friendly to strangers; American food with Italian influence - clean, basic, inexpensive and plentiful; neighborhood crowd spans all ages and social strata.

Michael's Waterfront, 85 Atlantic Ave, 367-6425
5:30 p.m.-10:30 p.m. Mon-Thurs; to 11 p.m. Fri & Sat; valet parking $5
Known for its rack of lamb; substantial portions; moderately priced; full wine

list from reasonable to expensive; decor - book-lined walls (mainly brick), which may account for the almost library-quiet atmosphere in the dining room; clientele mostly professional, upscale 30/40 somethings.

Boston Sail Loft, 80 Atlantic Ave, 227-7280
11:30 a.m-2 a.m. 7 days, 363 days a year; food served until 11 p.m.
Parking lot next door
Large portions, low to medium cost depending on whether you want a burger with fries and slaw ($5.50) or a fried fisherman's platter ($15.95); great desserts rivaled only by the great view of Boston Harbor and beyond; half-price appetizers Mon-Thurs from 4:30-6:30 p.m.; lively young crowd who don't mind standing in line to get in (Fridays and Saturdays in Spring and Summer); jars filled with "the real" Oreo cookies (no Hydrox here) placed every 15 feet or so on the lengthy bar, there for the taking one by one or by handfuls.

Cornucopia On The Wharf, 100 Atlantic Ave, 367-0300
5:30 p.m.-9:30 p.m. Sun-Thurs, to 10 on Fri & Sat, bar to midnight; open for lunch
Valet Parking Fri & Sat $7, adjacent parking lot $7, or on Commercial Street $3
"New American" food with traditional New England flavor - 60% seafood; menus change seasonally; true to its name, plentiful servings; entrees range from $13 to $20, probably more for the New England Steamed Lobster Supper whose price changes with the tides; favored by slightly older "yuppies"; casual but elegant; spectacular water view.

Jasper's, 240 Commercial St, 523-1126
5 p.m.-9 p.m. Tues-Fri, to 10 Sat; valet parking $8
Once the very best of Boston dining and among the most expensive, but word is out lately that Chef/Owner Jasper White, a culinary icon, may be slipping a tad. Some feel he has sacrificed quality and quantity to lower his prices, yet a three-course meal for two without beverages still hits nearly $100. Fair notice - think twice about making complaints or sending something back; Jasper doesn't take criticism well.

Waterview Restaurant, 150 Northern Ave, 357-8121
11 a.m to 1 a.m. 7 days; parking next door in Paul's Lobster lot
Formerly an abandoned warehouse metamorphosed into a beautiful,

open space with high ceilings and a brilliant chandelier reflecting in a grand mirror; "home of the Broiled Twin Lobsters"; reasonably priced; abundant portions; in season—outside dining deck overlooking the water; free appetizers with drinks in lounge; diverse clientele; unpretentious and relaxed atmosphere.

Daily Catch, 261 Northern Ave, 338-3093
11:30 a.m.-11 p.m. Mon-Sat, noon-11 Sun; no reservations; cash only
Seafood with an Italian accent; a good place for fresh fish at low to moderate prices but just to eat, not dine; fairly devoid of charm and missing the local color of the original in the North End.

Anthony's Pier 4, 140 Northern Ave, 482-6262
11:30 a.m.-11 p.m. 7 days (seats until 10)
The wait for a table is interminable, the service is less than adequate and the food isn't much better, but it's Boston's favorite tourist trap and every world-class city should have at least one. On the plus side, it has an awesome view of the harbor and Boston's skyline, an astounding wine list, giant popovers to fill up on while waiting (and waiting) for dinner, and free parking.

Jimmy's HarborSide, 242 Northern Ave, 423-1000
Noon to 9:30 p.m. Mon-Sat, opens at 4 Sun, lounge to 11; valet $3
Another Boston institution (more than 70 years old) but still drawing a large local crowd in addition to tourists; lobster lovers can pick from eight different kinds of preparations; lounge features a saxophone player on Fri & Sat and is a pleasant place to wait for your table, inevitable on weekends even with reservations if you're not a local luminary or national celebrity.

On The Water

Odyssey Cruises, Rowes Wharf, 654-9710
Every night in the summer, sporadically in the winter
A sailing you will go if you don't mind spending big bucks—$68.88 pp Sun-Thurs, $81.18 pp Fri & Sat for dining, wining and dancing for three hours on a world-class ship cruising around Boston Harbor.

BOSTON BY NIGHT

Spirit of Boston, Rowes Wharf, 569-4449
Sails from mid-to-late April through New Year's Eve
A three-hour tour Gilligan should have taken; lobster clambake June-Sept,
beef/chicken etc. buffet other months; a narration about Boston Harbor,
live entertainment and dancing for $45.95 Sun-Thurs, $48.90 Fri, $54.95 Sat.

LATE ENTRIES

Tavern On The Water, #1 Pier Six, Charlestown Navy Yard, 242-0050
5 p.m.-11 p.m. Mon-Sat, 5:30 p.m.-9 p.m. Sun, bar open to 1 a.m.; also
serves lunch; opened spring, '94;
Perched at the end of the pier, this tri-level American bistro is as close to
the water as you can get without a boat and still stay dry. Comfortably
furnished decks, some canopied, some open, extend out to the water,
affording a sweeping, unhampered view of the harbor, particularly from
the upper decks. An interior restaurant with an open grill, seating 20-30 is
planned for the first level. On the outer decks, cold foods and a raw bar
will be offered as well as a Sunset Jazz Series on Thurs & Fri 6 p.m.-11 p.m.
Another indoor bar and table seating for about 25 on second level
(already in operation), serving varied dishes heavy on seafood, yet the
steak was one of the best, most tender I have had anywhere; entrees $9-
$15; casual dress. Valet parking will be available for $3 for 3 hours at
Flagship Wharf, but the best, most fun way to get there is by water shuttle
from Long Wharf, particularly in fine weather.

Eurosia, Boston Park Plaza Hotel, Arlington St, (Back Bay), 542-1616
Opened late April, '94
A new venture by the owner of Mr Leung (see **RESTAURANT/ BACK BAY**
listing under **Asian**), more moderately priced and more versatile (Thai,
Chinese, etc.), Western style; open kitchen; attractively decorated; large
bar area ideally situated to become a hangout for locals and an end-
of-business day respite for hotel guests.

Pignoli's, 91 Park Plaza (Back Bay), 338-7500
Opening June, '94
Name suggests Italian food but probably, according to the manager, will
fall into the same category as Biba (see **BACK BAY RESTAURANT** listing

under **Continental**), same owner, classified as continental. There will also be a bakery. Most recent predecessors in this location have failed fairly quickly, but canny chef/owner Lydia Shire has the know-how, the following and, undoubtedly, the financial backing to succeed.

Ambrosia, 116 Huntington Ave, 723-9173
Opening June, '94, Mediterranean food
By definition, ambrosia is "anything that tastes or smells delicious." That's a good enough reason for choosing that as the name for a new restaurant, but a better one is when your own name is Ambrose, Tony that is, another alumnus of the Bostonian Hotel kitchen which has given us about a half dozen other leading culinary lights. Ambrosia should swiftly join the ranks of Boston's top restaurants given the owner's credentials and reputation.

Planet Hollywood, Quincy Market
A space problem may shoot down this star-studded eatery, scheduled to descend on Boston late spring or early summer, '94. The problem has something to do with low ceilings that don't conform to building codes. Very tall co-owner Arnold Schwarzenegger may feel this is a good enough reason to terminate the operation, but so far no one has yelled "Cut!".

CLUBS, LOUNGES, TAVERNS AND PUBS

Boston's night scene is very much like New England weather, changing all the time with very little notice, if any. What's "in" and "hot" one week could fade into oblivion the next. To stay at the peak of popularity, club and bistro owners are constantly changing formats, coming up with new themes, refurbishing, and generally switching gears faster than the weekly calendar listings can keep up with them. Unarguably, there are some very distinct lines drawn in age, status and economics as to who goes where on a given night. For the avant garde this is very serious business. Yet, for those who place no importance on being at the right place at the right time with the "right" people and just want to have fun, Boston offers myriad nightly delights. Desire to enjoy a night on the town is the only prerequisite for getting into the swing. The energy is high, the music is hot, and there's something for everyone.

If you have no terpsichorean talents nor tendencies, try some of the Irish pubs. They're congenial, filled with fun people of all ages, and great places to make friends out of strangers. Lounges are ideal for becoming reacquainted with your mate or getting to know a first date. Then there are those who prefer not to talk to each other, so go for the comedy clubs or the blues and jazz clubs where conversation is superfluous. Beats vegetating in front of the TV by a longshot. For the more athletically inclined, there are upscale billiard halls and an indoor miniature golf course, bowling alleys and arcades, and other activities where prowess takes a back seat to the spirit of adventure, lying just below the surface of even the most fainthearted. **No Cover Charge Unless Noted**

BACK BAY

*Dick's Last Resort, 55 Huntington Ave, 267-8080
Dancing to live music (8:15 p.m.-1:15 a.m. nightly) if you can hear it over the din of the earthy, boisterous (very young) crowd or if the tyrant at the door lets you in (all part of its unique style and charm); food to 2 a.m. (see **RESTAURANT** listing under **BACK BAY** American).

Hard Rock Cafe, 131 Clarendon St, 424-7625
Parking next door—no validation

Canned and live music, mostly local talent; dancing (if you can find room); the free-and-21 crowd; food (see **BACK BAY RESTAURANT** listing under **American**).

*Dad's Beantown Diner, 911 Boylston St, 296-DADS
Live music on Sun, DJ Mon-Sat, from 9 p.m-2 a.m; dancing
Dad may feel at home in the '50s decor with photos of classic film stars adorning the walls but, most likely, a bit out of place with the crowd (mostly 20's); full food service to 10 p.m., pizza to 2 a.m.

Daisy Buchanan's, 204A Newbury St, 247-8516
DJ Wed-Sat starting at 9 or 10 p.m.; juke box always; comedy night Wed 10 p.m.-1 a.m. (free); free buffet 4 p.m.-7 p.m. Thurs & Fri; cash only
A corner, neighborhood bar in a nice neighborhood attracting a mixed crowd; no dance floor, but that doesn't stop patrons moved by the beat; food in CIAOBELLA located above, an Italian restaurant, same owner, serving to 11 Mon-Wed, to 11:45 Thurs-Sun (Valet after 5 p.m. $8).

Club Nicole, 40 Dalton St (in the Back Bay Hilton), 267-2582
10:30 p.m.-2 a.m. Tues & Thurs-Sat; valet or garage $8-$10; cover $10-$12
A chic, New York style club catering to the monied, transcontinental set; Tuesdays are special theme nights with appropriate entertainment; International nights Thurs & Sat, Oriental Night Fri.

Library Grill Lounge, 84 Beacon St (in the Hampshire House), 227-9600
Valet $7
Curl up with a good...jazz trio from 7:30 p.m.-10:15 p.m. Thurs-Sun

Top of the Hub, Prudential Building, 52nd floor, 536-1775
Bar open 11 a.m.-12:15 a.m.. Sun-Thurs, to 1:15 Fri & Sat; validated parking in Prudential garage, free after 5 p.m.
Pianist Tues & Wed; jazz trioThurs-Sat starting at 9 p.m.; contemporary American regional food in dining room to 10 p.m. Sun-Thurs, to 11 p.m. Fri & Sat; an awsome view in a refined setting.

*Division Sixteen, 955 Boylston St, 353-0870
To 2 a.m. nightly

Development in this former police station has been arrested—no more live music but worth a mention for its drinks, so large a little person could bathe in them; full menu served to 1:30 a.m.

The Boston Park Plaza Hotel, 64 Arlington St, 426-2000
Swans Court 7:30 p.m.-11:30 p.m. Tues-Sat; validated valet parking $5 for 3 hours
Two shows at once here—the suave Jackson & Palter performing jazz and cabaret music, and people-watching from this open space located in the rear of one of the busiest, prettiest hotel lobbies in town.
Captain's Bar 3 p.m.-1 a.m. weekdays, 2 p.m.-1:30 a.m. weekends
Recently refurbished (April, '94) with a nautical theme for landlubbers looking for an intimate, cozy setting; jazz trio Thurs & Fri, 5:30-7:30 p.m., Sat 9 p.m.-Midnight

Copley Plaza Hotel, 138 St. James St., 267-5300
Plaza Bar 5 p.m-midnight Mon-Sat; valet parking $6
Sophisticated rhythm provided by a talented cabaret pianist/singer in a cosmopolitan setting; for the urbane and well dressed.

Sheraton Hotel & Towers, 39 Dalton St, 236-2000
*A Steak in the Neighborhood, 262-1822: free valet after 5 p.m.
DJ and dancing 10 p.m.-1:30 a.m. nightly; late night snacks to 1 a.m; locals and hotel guests of varying ages but predominantly 20's/30's; open for all three meals daily.
Turning Point Lounge, 3:30 p.m.-midnight nightly; valet parking $12 1-3 hours
For those who like conversation along with their entertainment (piano bar); casual and comfortable for the mostly over-30 crowd.

Westin Hotel, 10 Huntington Ave, 262-9600
Valet Parking $9 for 2 hours
Turner Fisheries, pianist Sun & Mon, live band Tues & Wed 8:30 p.m.-1 a.m.; pianist and singer Thurs, Fri & Sat 9:30 p.m.-1 a.m.; bar snacks available; settled crowd in pretty setting.
Lobby Lounge, pianist Thurs, Fri & Sat 3 p.m.-1 a.m.; spacious, gracious and comfortable.

Four Seasons Hotel, 200 Boylston St, 338-4400
Valet parking $8 first hour, $4 for each half hour thereafter, $18 maximum
*Bristol Lounge As sweet an evening as you could want—Viennese Dessert
Buffet (Fri & Sat 9 p.m.- 12:30 a.m.) and a jazz quartet to entertain you as your
hips grow ($8.75 for two desserts, four for $17.50, beverages not included).

Eliot Hotel, 370 Commonwealth Ave, 262-1078
The Eliot Lounge, Noon-2 a.m. daily
A sports bar (with big-screen TV) cum dance club on weekends—live
bands or DJ Fri & Sat from 9 p.m. ($3 cover) when the young outnumber the
varied-age sports enthusiasts who frequent the bar the rest of the week.

The Marriott Copley Place, 110 Huntington Ave, 236-5800
Parking Tip: After 5 p.m. you can park in adjoining Copley Place Garage
for $2 until 2 a.m. if you get your ticket validated from one of the stores in
the shopping complex; valet parking at the hotel costs $10 for 3 hours
(which could be cheaper in the end if you have to buy something you
don't need to get your ticket validated in a store).
*Champion's Sports Bar & Restaurant, 578-0658
11:30 a.m.-1 or 1:30 a.m. Sun-Thurs
Full menu and breakfast served to 3:30 a.m. Fri & Sat
You barely have to turn your head to watch TV in this rambling place with
20 big-screens and a 100 incher broadcasting sporting events (via three
satellites) including all title fights. For the non-sports fans, there's music provided
by a DJ, and dancing nightly; varied age group with the accent on youth.
Lobby Lounge, 11 a.m.-1:30 a.m; live bands and dancing Fri & Sat; open,
airy, and comfortable for the over 35 set.

Lenox Hotel, 710 Boylston St, 421-4900
Diamond Jim's, 8 p.m.-1 a.m Tues-Sat; free valet parking
Appetizers and snacks to midnight
An intimate, inviting lounge where the servers really rather sing and do,
and you can grab your ten minutes of spotlight on open-mike nights
acccompanied by a talented pianist who can provide vocal harmony if
requested—Tues, Fri & Sat, $2 cover; guest jazz/cabaret performers Wed
& Thurs, $6 cover; patrons range from 20's to golden age.

BRIGHTON/ALLSTON/BROOKLINE

Cafe Grappa, 1234 Soldiers Field Rd, 254-4336 (in the Days Inn)
7:30 p.m.-2 a.m. nightly; free parking
Pub by day, club by night; only the four large TVs to watch on Sun & Mon; music (1940s-'60s) kicks off on Tues with "Swingles' Night; top 40's on Wed, Fri, Sat; live blues on Thurs; dancing; crowd is a mixture of those looking for love and those who have already found it.

Rivermore Ballroom, 1234 Soldiers Field Rd, 254-4336 (in the Days Inn)
9 p.m.-2 a.m. Fri & Sat; free parking
Room to spread out on its 65-foot dance floor and sufficient seating for those with two left feet; various international themes, Latin or African or...., and many of the multi-ethnic, varied-age patrons come dressed appropriate to the theme; dinner and snacks available from Bennino's menu (see **RESTAURANT** listing); dinner theatre on Sunday nights.

Yelena, 298 Washington St, Brighton, 787-0037
Saturdays—live music and dancing; (see **RESTAURANT** listing under BRIGHTON Russian).

Local 186, 186 Harvard Ave, Allston, 351-2660
9 p.m.-2 a.m. nightly; cover $6-$8
Boston's grunge mecca (for now, anyway); live bands of varying tempos from hard rock to reggae for the young and hearty; features up-and-coming bands, some have made it big; two levels with four bars; dancing.

Great Scott, 1222 Commonwealth Ave, Brighton, 566-9014
Live alternative bands Fri & Sat 10 p.m.-2 a.m ($5 cover); the young and the restless dance to the juke box or the house sound system the rest of the week with time out for dart games and various other activities that change weekly.

Paradise, 969 Commonwealth Ave, Brighton, 254-3939
Wed-Sat 7 p.m.-11 p.m; cover $3-$15; valet after 11 p.m. $8
The flip side of M-80, ending when M-80 starts at 11 p.m.; live rock bands; recently renovated and expanded; the 20-something crowd.

M-80, 969 Commonwealth Ave, Brighton, 351-2527
Wed, Fri & Sat 11 p.m.-2 a.m; cover $10; valet $8
The other side of Paradise, the club that is; sort of ancient Roman/Grecco in decor and global musically; dance on lower level (DJ), relax in lounge on second floor; semi-private (which makes it even harder for the hoi polloi to get in); mainly international, well-heeled B.U., B.C. and Simmons students.

Blackbird Baking Company, 1032 Comm. Ave, (before Harvard St), Brighton, 739-9755
11:30 a.m.-11 or 11:30 p.m., Tues-Sat food to 10; reservations for large groups only
A funky, colorfully decorated place serving up live acoustic jazz along with "creative" American food (entrees $10-$16), wine, and beer to the 20's/30's crowd who rather listen than dance.

Armadillo Cafe, 1314 Comm. Ave, Brighton, 232-4242
5 p.m.-10 p.m. Mon-Wed, 11:30 a.m.-1 a.m Thurs-Sat, noon to midnight Sun
Strolling mariachi bands Wed; guitarist/singer Fri & Sat at dinner hours then live pop bands starting at 10 p.m.

Silhouette Lounge, 200 Brighton Ave, Allston, 254-9306
11:30 a.m.-1 a.m. nightly, opens at noon on Sun; cash only
Comes out of the shadows on Thurs & Sat with live jazz/blues starting at 9 p.m. ($2 cover); free comedy night Sun with local talent, both professional and amateur; juke box rest of the week.

Tam O'Shanter, 1648 Beacon St, Brookline, 277-0982
To 2 a.m. Sun-Fri, to 1 a.m. Sat; food served to 10
Everything but bag pipes here seven nights a week, starting at 10 p.m.; live bands (and dancing) ranging from R&B to calypso; most of the lads and lassies are in their 20's.

O'Brien's Pub, 3 Harvard Ave, Allston, 782-6245
10 a.m.-1 a.m. daily; cash only
A pub for sure, but not Irish despite its name; live bands Fri & Sat varying from week to week, from Country to Rock 'n Roll; no dancing, no food, just serious drinking for the college to 40 set.

BOSTON BY NIGHT

Tuesday's Ice Cream, 30 Station St, Brookline, 566-8190
Jazz for the whole family here where toasting is done with ice cream
sodas or milk shakes—Thurs & Sun 7-9 p.m. spring and summer.

Green Briar, 304 Washington St, Brighton, 789-4100
9:30-1 a.m. nightly; live rock 'n roll bands Mon, Fri & Sat, Irish band Wed,
also live bands Fri & Sat at 4:30 p.m.; cover $3-$5; food, fun and games
for all but no dancing.

The Kels, 161 Brighton Ave, Allston, 782-9082
An Irish pub with a conglomeration of live and canned entertainment, both
Irish and mainstream, beginning on Mon with Comedy night (10 p.m.-1 a.m.),
a solo musician on Tues, a mixed bag of live bands Wed-Sat, and a DJ
on Sun (9:30 p.m.-1:30 a.m.); dancing Wed-Sun; $3 cover on Fri & Sat.

O'Leary's, 1010 Beacon St, Brookline, 734-0049
11 a.m.-12:45 a.m. daily
A pub with true Irish temperament—fun loving; live traditional Irish music
Sat 9 p.m.-12:45 a.m. & Sun 8-11:30 p.m.; food.

Kinvara Pub, 34 Harvard Ave, Allston, 783-9400
10 a.m.-2 a.m Mon-Sat, opens at noon Sun; $3 cover Fri & Sat after 9 p.m.
Free parking in rear lot
Live rock 'n roll bands Wed-Sat 9 p.m-2 a.m., Irish band Sun 4-8 p.m., DJ 9 p.m-
2 a.m.; mixed neighborhood crowd Irish and otherwise.

The Boyne, (formerly Stadium Restaurant/Pub), 458 Western Ave, Brighton, 782-2418
8 a.m.-2 a.m. Mon-Sat, opens at noon on Sun, cash only
Named after a river in Ireland, so the live Irish bands (Fri & Sat, sometimes
Sun & Thurs) naturally go with the flow; mixed crowd, dancing.

CAMBRIDGE

A vibrant, dynamic city just across the Charles River from Boston, Cambridge
is deserving (and would require) an ...After Dark book all its own. Here are
a few of the most distinctive clubs/restaurants for which Bostonians are

willing, indeed eager, to deal with the frustrations of heavy traffic and limited free parking to enjoy the spirit of "The Free Republic of Cambridge."

Averof, 1924 Massachusetts Ave (Porter Square), 354-4500
5 p.m.- 1 a.m. Sun-Sat; bar open to 2 a.m. weekends; open for lunch; valet $3
The most fun you can have in public without getting into trouble with the law, this place just oozes with excitement. The Middle Eastern food is good but not spectacular ($8-$13), but the live bands (nightly), belly dancers (Sat & Sun) and infectious sense of joie de vivre are the main reasons for coming here. Archetypal owner/host Raymond embraces (figuratively for first timers, literally for repeaters) everyone who crosses his threshold. The international set takes over around 10 when most of the Americans leave. Definitely worth the 15-minute ride from Boston.

House of Blues, 96 Winthrop St, 491-2583
The brainstorm of Hard Rock Cafe founder Isaac Tigrett with such celebrity investors as actor Dan ("Blues Brothers") Aykroyd, the first of many to be opened (Fall, '92) around the country; a converted town house with Southern folk art and ceiling reliefs of blues heroes; credited for strengthening Greater Boston's blues scene. (See **Blues Clubs**)

Middle East Restaurant/Club/Cafe, 472 Mass. Ave, 354-8238
Most well known as a jazz club but also often features underground alternative bands (See **Jazz Clubs**)

Ryles, 212 Hampshire St, 876-9330 (See **Jazz Clubs**)

Regattabar, Charles Hotel, 1 Bennett St, 937-4020 (See **Jazz Clubs**)

Western Front, 343 Western Ave, 492-7772
5 p.m.-1 a.m. Tues & Wed, to 1:30 Thurs, to 2 Fri-Sun
Cover $5 Tues-Thurs, $10 Fri-Sun; free parking
Dingy and dark but glowing with the spirit of reggae and jazz bands featured here regularly. Taking a complete 360 degree turn, it becomes the Arts Cafe on Sunday night featuring performance arts and poetry, comedy and music.

BOSTON BY NIGHT

Man-Ray, 21 Brookline St (Central Square), 864-0400
9 p.m-2 a.m. Wed-Sat; $3 cover most nights; cash only
One of the few clubs in the area that offers industrial alternative music
most of the time. Patrons are requested to come in "creative dress" and
most choose punk style, mainly black and shod in Doc Martins, to blend in
with the dark, Gothic decor; 18+ most nights.
Campus: The brighter side of Man-Ray, sometimes set aside for gentlemen who prefer gentlemen (See **Alternative Life Styles**).

Paradise Cafe, 180 Mass Ave, 864-4130 (See **Alternative Life Styles**)

The Toad, 1912 Mass. Ave (Porter Square), 497-4950
5 p.m.-1 a.m. Sun-Wed, to 2 a.m. Thurs-Sat
Live bands and dancing every night from 10 p.m. for the young and hearty.

TT The Bear's Place, 10 Brookline St, 492-0082 (Central Square)
To 1 a.m. nightly, opens at 4 p.m. Mon-Fri, at 6 p.m. Sat, at 2 p.m. Sun;
cover varies
Alternative bands Tues-Sat 9 p.m-1 a.m. ($4-$8); spoken word performance
by Stone Soup Poetry Group Mon 8-11 p.m. ($3); dance floor but few
dance; Ethiopian food served only on Sun to accommodate the large Ethiopian community in that area; pool tables (75 cents per game); mixed crowd.

DOWNTOWN BOSTON

Custom House Lounge, Bay Tower Room, 60 State St, 723-1666
Pianists 5:30 p.m.-7:30 p.m. Mon & Tues and 5:30 p.m.-8:30 p.m.
Thurs & Fri; quartet 5 p.m.-9 p.m. Wed; swing band 9 p.m.-1 a.m. Fri & Sat;
validated garage parking
Urbane and gracious with a panoramic view from the 33rd floor; a
comfortable environment for the over-40 set; dancing; "proper dress"
requested. (see **RESTAURANT** listing under **DOWNTOWN** for dining information).

The Last Hurrah, 60 School St (in Omni Parker Hotel), 227-8600
DJ and dancing Thurs-Sat 7:30 p.m.-12:30 a.m. (Friday is Oldies night) in a
clubby setting for "older" folks (over 30).

The Littlest Bar, 47 Province St, 523-9766
8 a.m.-1 a.m. 7 days
Room for around 20 people (but often packed with more); sing along with the hosts of "Monday Night Madness;" Irish band every Thurs; a quieter, nifty little watering hole the rest of the week.

West Street Grille, 15 West St, 423-0300
The home of the swingiest of Boston's young swingers; Monday is "Cafe Au Lait" night from 10 p.m.-2 a.m. when Latin lovers can lombardo their hearts out free (no cover) if they can find room on the makeshift dance floor; other nights vary from week to week when dancing is not discouraged, but you may have to tiptoe through the tables since the dance floor disappears until the next Monday; dancing, however, is not a priority to the swarm of regulars who have other activities in mind. The second floor with the fireplace and quiet little bar is roped off for the A-List when the first-floor bar is bulging with the not-so-elite; food (see **RESTAURANT/Downtown** listing).

Province Street Pub, 18 Province St, 227-2992
11:30 a.m.-2 a.m Mon-Sat, opens at noon on Sunday; validated parking $3
A two-level pub with a U-shaped bar and loft dining room; live bands, varying styles, Fri & Sat; mixed crowd.

Metropolis, 533 Washington St, 338-6999
As of this writing, still in process of renovation and due to reopen in late Spring, '94; owner promises a sleek new look for this three-floor club that failed as "The Hub," some say because of its location close to "The Combat Zone", which leads us to the.......

Naked I Cabaret, 666 Washington St, 426-7462
11 a.m.-2 a.m Mon-Sat, opens at noon on Sun
Much more than the "I" is naked at this "never-a-cover" joint (speaking both literally and figuratively), among the very few left in what remains of Boston's "Combat Zone." Decide for yourself if it's worth a sojurn to this disreputable area for "the most beautiful girls in Boston," according to its own claims.

BOSTON BY NIGHT

FENWAY/KENMORE SQUARE

The hub of the city's dance clubs catering largely to hip Generation X-ers and the International set, but "mainstreamers" (the unhip, who may or may not be aware of being labelled as such) are beginning to assert their presence, standing their ground in the face of selective keepers of the doors. With Fenway Park (just a homerun away from the Kenmore "T" stop), sports bars also proliferate here, drawing the sports oriented seeking the simpatico to watch and rehash Red Sox games.

Rathskeller - "The Rat," 528 Commonwealth Ave, 536-2750
Valet parking $5; cover $5-$7
Lots of Harleys outside and leather inside; live rock & roll bands 9:30 p.m.-2 a.m. Wed-Sat; dancing.

Copperfield's, 98 Brookline Ave, 247-8605
Cover $4; free garage parking across the street after 7 p.m.
Live rock 'n roll bands Wed-Sat 9 p.m.-2 a.m.; dancing.

Avalon, 15 Lansdowne St, 262-2424
10 p.m.-2 a.m. Thurs ($10), 9:30 p.m.-2 a.m. Fri & Sat ($8), 9 p.m.-2 a.m. Sun ($6); special events other nights; free Fri & Sat from 9:30-10:30 and Sun from 9-10 (if you can get by the lines in time); valet parking $8; no athletic wear on Thurs, no sneakers on Fri, collared shirts required on Sat, no ripped jeans ever. Each night here is different ranging from International (Thurs), Latin Salsa (Fri), Top 40 (Sat) to Alternative Lifestyles (Sun), all complimented by state-of-the-art light and sound systems; a plushly decorated, ballroom style entertainment facility with 14 full-service bars, intimate booths, and a lounge for quieter moments.

Axis/DV8, 13 Lansdowne St, 262-2437
10:30 p.m-2 a.m. Tues ($6), Thurs ($7 for 21+, $10 for 18+) and Sun ($5), 10 p.m.-2 a.m. Wed ($6), Fri ($6 for 21+, $10 for 19+), and Sat ($7)
Turning constantly; two floors with spacious dance floor and eight full bars; self-described as "Bold as Love;" creative dress (but no hats, hoods or sneakers), tailored to whatever may be happening on a given night which

could be anything (heavy metal, techno, '70s soul, etc); Sundays are reserved for Alternative Lifestyles; second-floor private room is called DV8 which offers billiard and foosball tables in a more intimate atmosphere.

Venus de Milo, 11 Lansdowne St, 421-9595
9 p.m.-2 a.m. nightly; no baseball caps or sneakers
This multi-level, classic Gothic ballroom with a spectacular chandelier was voted twice ('90 and '91) by <u>Boston Magazine</u> as "Best Nightclub" and is among the most popular with Boston's dynamic young crowd; nine full bars and a sufficient variety of live and canned music to appeal to everyone short of the Tony Bennett set; Sunday is for the Euro crowd ($6); Monday, a hodgepodge of entertainment with a weekly theme ($3); Phatt Tuesday ($4); Wednesday, Alternative Lifestyles ($4); Thursday, Techno ($5); Friday, Jam Central Station - top 40s ($7); Saturday Night Fever '70s disco ($7).

Bill's Bar & Lounge, 7 Lansdowne St, 421-9678
9 p.m.-2 a.m. nightly
An arm of the Venus De Milo and just as diverse in its musical offerings starting with Reggae on Sundays ($6) and ending the week (Saturdays) with classic new wave ($2); in between there are a couple of no-cover nights - Mondays, movies and popcorn, and Fridays - rock 'n roll to the jukebox; Tues & Wed (live bands) - $4, Thurs (DJ) - $5; roadhouse style and ambience.

Jake Ivory's, 1 Lansdowne St, 247-1222
8 a.m.-2 a.m. Wed-Sat; $4 cover Wed & Thurs, $5 Fri & Sat
Dueling pianists (4 players) with an endless repertoire of songs going from rock 'n roll to standards to show tunes, etc. etc., helped along vocally by enthusiastic audiences.

Quest, 1270 Boylston St, 424-7747
9 p.m.-2 a.m. Mon, Wed, Sat; 10 p.m.-2 a.m. Tues, Thurs, Fri, Sun
No sneakers, athletic wear or hats
Formerly strictly gay gone straight for half the week (Tues, techno - $5; Thurs, top 40 - $5; Fri, Int'l Disco/College - $7 for 21+, $10 for 19+; Sun, International - $10); gay nights are Mon (house music - $1), Wed, (dance music - $4) and Sat (house music - $5); mostly DJs, sometimes live bands;

three floors representing different environments, from earth to water to fire, and a roof deck appropriately representing air; dramatic, avant garde and stylish; two bars on each of the 1st, 2nd and roof levels and three on the 3rd.

Best Western Boston Lounge, 342 Longwood Ave, 731-4700
Garage parking $12
DJ and dancing Fri, 5 p.m-midnight.
Close to a concentration of hospitals so mainly hotel guests looking for some distraction from visiting hospitalized family or friends.

Maxwell Jumps, 335 Huntington Ave, 266-1705
To 2 a.m.; $3 cover at whim (when busy, live music, etc.)
DJ Thurs, Fri, Sat beginning between 8 & 9 p.m.; dancing; live music on occasion; college crowd (across from Northeastern U.).

Who's on First, 23 Yawkey Way (Fenway Park) 247-3353
To 2 a.m. nightly with varying opening hours according to whether the Red Sox are in town
No, this is not an Abbot and Costello routine, but a sports bar with entertainment and dancing on weekends ($2-$8 cover but free to those who show ticket stubs from the Sox game); simple pub food for under $5; strictly a jeans and sneakers kind of place.

FINANCIAL DISTRICT

Il Panino, 275 Franklin St., 338-1000
Valet parking $7
Jazz Club Wed. - Sat., 9 p.m.-2 a.m.
Dad could double date with his son and neither would feel out of place here; live swing music; dancing.
Dance Club Fri & Sat, 9 p.m.-2 a.m.
John Travolta strikes again - disco provided by a DJ; 20's and 30's primarily but some feisty 40's and nifty 50's; no cover except on very busy Fridays and Saturdays when $10 lets you roam from one to the other in this stylish four-level restaurant/entertainment complex (See **RESTAURANTS, FINANCIAL DISTRICT,** Italian).

Schooners Oyster Bar & Grill, 200 High St, 261-9960
6 p.m.-2 a.m. Thrus, Fri, Sat; free valet parking on Sat
Blues on Thursdays unless the house band has another gig in which case you'll have to settle for canned disco music; Greek music Fridays (starting at 10) and Saturdays (starting at 11); $10 minimum for either food or drink; also a restaurant serving Greek food on Sat night and American/seafood the rest of the week.

Three Cheers Restaurant & Bar, 290 Congress St, 423-6166
8 p.m-2 a.m; validated parking in lot next door
Looks more like the famed "Cheers" bar than the Bull & Finch after which the now-defunct TV show was fashioned; karaoke Thursdays, dancing to a DJ Fridays; 25-40-year olds; restaurant serves from 11:30 a.m.-11 p.m. (American food).

Bakey's Bar & Restaurant, 45 Broad St, 426-1710
11:30 a.m.-10 p.m. Mon-Fri weekdays
A deli bar turned jazz club on Thursday nights 6-10 p.m. - live jazz band.

JAMAICA PLAIN

Brendan Behan Pub, 378 Centre St, 522-5386
Noon-1 a.m. 7 days; cash only
A favorite, neighborhood hangout but an ever-increasing number of encroachers are discovering why the locals have such a good time here. In addition to the overall ambience, there are live bands Mon, Wed & Sun 10 p.m.-1 a.m., live Irish traditional music Tues 8 p.m. -1 a.m., and (I kid you not) poetry readings either on Tues or Sat, all without any cover charge, ever. With drinks ranging from only $2-$4, this may be the best deal around.

NORTH STATION

Commonwealth Brewing Co., 138 Portland St, 523-8383
Live reggae/blues bands 9:30 p.m.-1 a.m. Fri & Sat; dancing; food (see RESTAURANTS American listing under NORTH STATION); $3 cover, waived if you have dinner.

Buck's American Bar and Grill, 197 Portland St, 248-9494
11:30 a.m.-10 p.m. Mon-Wed, to 2 a.m. Thurs-Sat
Cosmopolitan, at least by North Station-area stardards (although things
are looking up there); live blues Thurs-Sat 9 p.m.-2 a.m.; no dancing but
eating - mainly grilled foods.

The Beanpot, 150 Canal St, 722-9321
9 a.m.-2 a.m. 7 days; usually no cover
A Boston Garden area rookie and already on its way to being an all-
star; a humongous restaurant/sports bar/nightclub offering contemporary
American food ($4-$10), about a dozen TVs, billiards, darts, keno and
video game room in addition to live bands Thurs-Sat.

Bullfinch Bar, 141 Portland St, 523-8640
10:30 a.m.-2 a.m.; cover $3-$5
A fun eatery with live music and dancing Fri & Sat (see **RESTAURANT/
NORTH STATION**, American).

Celebrities, 262 Friend St, 723-2288
11 a.m.-2 a.m. 7 days
First-floor sports bar with seven TVs; holds around 200 people; music and
dancing sometimes; Ambassador Club planned for third floor (opening
summer, '94) geared toward the mid-twenties crowd - live bands and/or
DJs planned, cover to be determined; Thai restaurant on second floor
serves to 10:30 (see **RESTAURANT** listings under **NORTH STATION**, Asian).

Paddy Burke's, 130 Portland St, 367-8370
Noon-2 a.m. 7 days; validated parking in Government Center Garage $4
This is truly a bit of the auld sod plunked down on its own private street, in
fact on Boston's smallest city block, inhabited soley by this four-story,
triangular-shaped building. The first floor is the traditional Irish pub; the
second is pub-like as well with TV screens where Irish soccer games and
the BBC news is transmitted live via satellite; third floor is for musical entertainment - live Irish bands Thurs-Sat; the fourth is the place for those who
want to play pool and video games while keeping an eye on the TV;
Irish version of a jam session (spelled the same but pronounced differ-
ently) Sun starting at 5 p.m. and continuing until closing or "when they fall

over and go home," whichever comes first; frequented principally by the over-30, Irish professional set from both sides of the Atlantic (accepts Irish currency and converts to dollars); cover only for special events such as an important soccer match direct from Ireland.

The Causeway, 65 Causeway St, 723-4565
9 p.m.-1:30 a.m. Tues-Sat; cash only; cover $5-$6
An Irish pub that had gone mainstream (offering local rock bands nightly) but as of this writing, by the wayside (closed). May reopen, but then again, it may not according to latest (non) information. Check on this one before going.

Harp at the Garden, 85 Causeway St, 742-1010
Cover $3 Thurs, $5 Fri & Sat
The Harp is hoppin' with live entertainment - Irish band Wed 7-11 p.m., rock 'n roll Thurs-Sat 10 p.m.-2 a.m., alternative Sun 9:30 p.m.-1 a.m.; dancing; food served to midnight.

Irish Embassy Pub, 234 Friend St, 742-6618
11 a.m.-2 a.m. 7 days; cover $3-$5 Fri & Sat
When the kitchen closes at 8, the music and dancing begin, to live Irish/ Rock bands. Appetizers are $1 when ordered along with a drink.

SOUTH END

Claddagh, 335 Columbus Ave, 262-9874
To 1 a.m. nightly; garage parking across the street $7
Irish in name, international in intention; live music (variously Irish, R&B and contemporary) and dancing Wed, Fri, Sat; food (see **RESTAURANT** listing American under **SOUTH END**).

Paramount, 965 Mass. Ave, 541-0101
9 p.m.-2 a.m.Thurs-Sun, cover varies
An upscale dance club, recently renovated, with jazz bar and Champagne VIP room; crowd changes according to the evening's theme— alternative life style on Thurs, Brazilian on Fri, African-American Sat, and Cape Verdian on Sun.

THEATRE DISTRICT

Located off Boylston Street about a block from the corner of Tremont Street, a dimly lit alley called Boylston Place is one of the city's brightest, hottest areas with a concentration of clubs, cafes and bistros offering a variety of entertainment options for all ages and stages. The Alley can also be reached from Stuart Street by crossing through the Transportation Building Food Court.

Zanzibar, Boylston Pl, 351-7000
Valet parking $8
This place could bring out the animal in you - two levels of jungle decor with palms and vines (for Tarzan, no doubt, should he decide to drop in); wear your dressy loin cloth; Tues International Night, 10:30 p.m.-2 a.m., $10, creative dress; Wed, 9 p.m.-2 a.m., Oldies Lost 45's with videos of the way we were, $5, casual attire; Thurs 9 pm.-2 a.m., '70s & '80s alternative, $5; Fri & Sat 9 p.m.-2 a.m., Top 40, $7, proper attire; dancing. Above Zanzibar is the **Crescent Club**, a clearing in the jungle - lounge/sitting room, 2 pool tables (takes quarters), juke box (entrance to both clubs for same cover charge); mainly 20's-40's crowd in both, but comfortable for any age.

Esmé, Boylston Place, 482-3399
9 p.m.-2 a.m. Thurs-Sat; special theme parties other nights; valet $8; cover $5-$10 Suggestive of a fashionable, European bawdy house and as much fun; buzzing bar, alcoves with couches, cafe tables, and roomy dance floor; discreetly lit for everyone to display themselves at best advantage; techno music (new-age word for disco); well-dressed crowd of all ages and stages; Sunday - for women who prefer women; Tuesday International night; bypass the line by dining first in sister restaurant, **Marais** (see RESTAURANT listing, **BACK BAY, THEATRE DISTRICT**).

Avenue C, Boylston Pl, 423-3832
9 p.m. to 2 a.m. Wed-Sat; no sneakers; cover Thurs-Sat $4 before 10, $8 after The street where students and young professionals live to dance, mix and mate; Wednesday is 18+ night when the under-legal-drinking agers pay $10 for techno music; progressive new wave Thurs-Sat; occasionally live bands.

Alley Cat, Boylston Pl, 351-2510
8 a.m.-2 a.m Wed & Sat, opens at 7 on Thurs & Fri; valet $9; $2 cover after 10
Purr-fect for hep cats still young enough to believe they have nine lives left; vivid graphics of such fuzzy favorites as Garfield and Felix adorn the walls; outrageous concoctions for the very tolerant, generally capped off by "slalom" shots; "cutting edge" karaoke on Wed, top 40's by DJ Thurs-Sat, CD juke box when he's not spinning, TV and foosball always; outdoor cafe in season.

Sweet Water Cafe, Boylston Pl, 351-2515
7 p.m.-2 a.m. Mon-Fri; opens at 3 p.m. Sat; valet $8; $2 cover Thurs-Sat
Even sweeter downstairs in "The Hangin' Tree," where they claim to have "the sexiest country bar this side of El Paso;" live bands on Thurs (reggae), Fri & Sat (country fried rock), jukebox the rest of the time; dancing; also a Tex-Mex restaurant and outside cafe (in season); the gathering place for Boston's young business set.

Sticky Mike's, Boylston Pl, 351-2540
See listing for **Blues Clubs**

The Roxy, 275 Tremont St (in the Tremont House Hotel), 227-7669;
9 p.m.-2 a.m. Fri, Sat, Sun; special events other nights
A pioneer in the rejuvination of Boston's nightlife, this grand, not-so-very-old lady has had a face lift and now beckons to a younger (20's/30's), more multi-cultural crowd; large with spacious dance floor and several bars so quaffers can quaff at will; private booths on the mezzanine with an aerial view of the abundant action below; International Night Fri; DJ with live entertainment Sat when the post-40 crowd still show up; Latin Night Sun; live boxing matches monthly with top-rank contenders; cover ranges from $5 to $25 depending on activity.

Juke Box/GALXC, 275 Tremont St (in the Tremont House Hotel), 542-1123
8 p.m.-2 a.m. Fri & Sat; two for the price of one ($5)
Juke Box: The ruling retro queen for the '50s/'60s decades with appropriate decor to bring that era back to life.
GALXC: More contemporary, playing top 40's with the focus on current video music.

8 Track, (formerly Playoff's), 100 Warrenton St, 426-0300
9 p.m.-2 a.m. Thurs-Sat
Neo disco ducks, who were only in elementary school during the shallow '70s, are keeping the feathers flying in this slick, new retro club with bean bag chairs, lava lamps and go-go cages; twirl to the BeeGees, Donna Summer and the rest of the '70s sounds provided by a DJ; occasional live entertainment; cover from $3-$5.

Europa, 51 Stuart St, 482-3939
9 p.m-2 a.m. Wed-Sun; cover varies
Another, large, hot, multi-cultural, two-level venue with dance club, jazz room and VIP bar; International Nights Wed & Sat; Americans take over on Fri and the Brazilians on Sun; special events other nights.

Roberta's Show-Biz Cafe, 76 Warrenton St (in the Charles Playhouse), 426-6339
5 p.m-2 a.m. Tues-Thurs, opens at 4 Fri-Sun; food until 11:30; closed Mondays
A nifty bistro for local and national theatrical types; perfect for pre- and post-theatre hobnobbing or to spend the whole evening; an intimate, New-York-style, supper-club setting with "creative cafe" food (served to midnight); live, sophisticated music for listening and/or dancing, and a piano bar to keep everything humming when the other performers take their breaks. Blond and pretty owner, Roberta, and her partner Gregg sure know how to keep their patrons happy.

Josephine's, 246 Tremont St (below the Wilbur Theatre), 426-4489
Named after Josephine Baker, this new club is offering, what else?, live jazz and blues nightly, in addition to a show (7-9 p.m.) called "Cole to Cole," Cole Porter classics as Nat King Cole would have performed them; cover $7-$25 depending on what's happening.

Charlie Flynn's, 228 Tremont St, 451-5997
11 a.m.-2 a.m. 7 days
A recent addition to Boston's nightlife conveniently located for pre- or post-theatre munching and/or quaffing; Thurs, Fri and Sat. (starting at 9 p.m.) variously DJ, live music or karaoke; dancing; free appetizers from 4 p.m.-7 p.m.

57 Restaurant Lounge, 200 Stuart St, 423-5700
8 p.m.-2 a.m. nightly
Sophisticated setting for over 40's; music and dancing Thurs-Sat.

Dominic's, 255 Tremont St, 426-8769
6 a.m.-2 a.m daily
Not your A-crowd but the B's and C's have fun there; DJ ('70s disco) Fri &
Sat 10 p.m.-2 a.m., jukebox rest of week; dancing; food.

WATERFRONT

Destinations, 1 Congress St, (Haymarket Square) 742-1212
Garage parking $5
It's all Greek to them—the food (from 11 a.m. weekdays, from 4 p.m. Sat &
Sun), the music (live), and the dancing (Thurs-Sun 10 p.m.-2 a.m.); a sleek
club with dim lights occasionally brightened by strobes; mostly couples of
all ages but chances are a girl's companion is her brother or her cousin
since Greek tradition calls for single young ladies to be properly escorted;
no dress code but regulars have their own standards of jackets, ties, and
cocktail dresses. Its **Night Owl Sports Bar** is an island in this Aegean sea of
delights, offering pool tables, dart boards and a big screen TV; and what
could be more sporting than lingerie shows (every Friday night).

Mirage, 1 Congress St, 742-1212 (upstairs from Destinations)
Someone's vision of eclectic and then some - Oil wrestling Wed (6 p.m,
$5), but don't bring your own lubricants, this is strictly for the pros (female);
Thurs is "Stocks and Bonds II" (name of owner's former club and not sug-
gestive of any hanky panky) with DJ/Disco (starting at 10, $3 cover); get out
the chaps for Fridays when it becomes "Boots" with country music (starting
at 8:30, $5 cover); Sat & Sun are Arabic Nights with live band and belly
dancer (starting at 9:30, no cover but $10 minimum spending requirement).
I'm exhausted just writing about it all.

Michael's Lounge, 85 Atlantic Ave., 367-6425
4 p.m.-1 a.m.; complimentary buffet Mon-Fri 4 p.m.-6:30 p.m.; valet parking $5
Table seating with separate bar area for easier mixing and matching; TVs

scattered everywhere, some large screen, for watching sporting events in a party atmosphere; pool table (no charge); relaxed and casual; 20's to 30's predominate with some young-looking 40's.

Perry's Saloon, 199 State St, 367-0303
To 2 a.m. nightly; validated parking at 75 State St; cover $4 Fri & Sat
The Beavis and Butt head crowd searching for love or any facsimile thereof; live band in bar upstairs Fri & Sat, dancing nightly downstairs to DJ (top 70's).

Tatsukichi, 189 State St, 720-2468
Parking across street $2
For singer wannabees—karaoke Mon-Sat 7 p.m.-1 a.m.; Japanese food (see **RESTAURANT** listings under **WATERFRONT**).

Sissy K's, 4 Commercial St, 248-6511
8:30 p.m.- 2 a.m. Fri & Sat in winter, Wed-Sun in summer
A bit seedy but hardly noticeable in the dim lights; DJ; dancing.

Dockside Restaurant & Bar, 183 State St, 723-7050
11:30-1 a.m. Sun-Thurs, to 2 a.m. Fri & Sat; validated parking at 75 State St $5
Sports bar (check out the photos of legendary sports figures that line the walls); karaoke Fridays; sing along with acoustic guitarist Sat, from 8:30 p.m.

Jose McIntyre's, 160 Milk St, 451-9460
11 a.m.-2 a.m. 7 days; no cover
A cafe with an identity crisis - Irish and Mexican in decor, ambience and food (inexpensive, served to 9 p.m.); live music Fri-Sun beginning at 9:30, juke box rest of the week; dancing any place you can find room; a place where construction workers and young professionals find common ground.

Nick's Tavern, 3 Lewis St, 523-9866
10:30 a.m. to 1 a.m. 7 days
A pint-sized bar (no pun intended) my mother would have called "a dive," but with a certain appeal that has sustained its popularity with the locals for over 70 years; occasional theme parties, ie Aruba Night featuring Caribbean music and food; good place to watch sporting events with others who share your enthusiasm.

Clarke's, 21 Merchant's Row, 227-7800
11:30 a.m.-2 a.m. 7 days; $2 off parking at 75 State St garage
Singer/guitarist Fri-Sun 9:30 p.m.-1 a.m.; patrons are welcome to sing along;
food served to 10 p.m. weekdays, 11 weekends; noisy, busy and bustling
most of the time with crowds that vary according to the hour (briefcase
crowd after work; younger, more casual later in evening and weekends).

Bostonian Hotel Atrium Lounge, 20 North St, 523-3600
Valet $12 for more than two hours
Elegant setting for the more mature; jazz pianist Tues-Sat 5 p.m.-12:30 a.m.,
joined by a young man on a horn Wed 6:30 p.m-10:30 p.m.

Rachel's in the Marriott Long Wharf, 296 State St, 227-0800
4 p.m.-2 a.m.; $5 cover; compulsory coat check at $1
DJ rarely diverting from "thump, thump" music; dancing; lots of ladies of the
evening, both professional and amateur, and leftovers from the more
trendy places, most of whom haven't a clue as to what's "in" or "out," and
probably don't care.

Boston Harbor Hotel Harbor View Lounge, 70 Rowes Wharf, 439-7000
3 p.m.-12:30 a.m. nightly; valet (after 5:30) $12, self park $7
Continental and capacious with a mesmerizing view of the harbor; one of
the best outdoor cafes in the city location wise; jazz trio Thurs-Sat 8:30
p.m.-12:30 a.m.; pianist everyday 3 p.m.-5 p.m. joined by a guitarist on Fri.

Green Dragon Tavern, 11 Marshall St, 367-0055
11 a.m.-2 a.m. Mon-Sun; cover $3
Live music nightly both rock and traditional starting at 9 p.m.; congenial
and noisy; all ages.

Purple Shamrock, 1 Union St, 227-2060
11:30 a.m.-2 a.m. 7 days; cover $3 Thurs-Sat
Green has given way to purple in this Irish pub where the neon shamrocks
cast a lavendar glow over an amiable, casual setting for all ages; live
music nightly.

BOSTON BY NIGHT

Black Rose, 160 State St, 742-2286
11 a.m.-2 a.m. daily; cover $5 Thurs-Sat
A true Irish pub where all ages and ethnic backgrounds can become
leprechauns for a night; Irish bands nightly beginning at 9:30 p.m.

Bell in Hand, 45 Union St, 227-2098
Noon-2 a.m. daily
Oldest tavern in the United States and still ringing with good cheer
despite the absence of live music or dancing.

Mr. Dooley's Tavern, 77 Broad St, 338-5656
11 a.m.-2 a.m. 7 days; Cover $2 Fri & Sat
St. Patty's night all year long where the blarney sometimes overpowers
the traditional music (nightly except Mon starting at 10); Irish version of jam
session Tues, Wed, Sun 7-10 p.m. when anyone can join in.

In Faneuil Hall Marketplace

Marketplace Cafe, Grill & Oar Bar, 300 North Market Bldg, 227-1272
Cafe, R&B band Tues-Thurs 8:30 p.m.-12:30 a.m
Oar Bar, live jazz band 9 p.m.-1 a.m. Fri & Sat; crowd here a little older
since it is mainly a restaurant (American/seafood) and serves until around 11 p.m.

Boston Beach Club, under Marketplace Cafe, 227-9664
9 p.m. to 2 a.m.
Surf on down here for live rock/pop music and dancing nightly; snacks
available to around 11 p.m.

Durgin-Park, 227-2038, North Market, street level
Piano player every night, some nights from 5-8 p.m., others from 6-10 p.m.;
live bands or DJs on Fri & Sat from 10 p.m.-1 a.m.

Lily's Famous Ribs/Lily's Cafe, North Canopy, 720-5580
Sun-Wed 11:30 a.m. to whenever depending on crowd, to 1:30 a.m. Thurs-Sat
Karaoke Fri & Sat from 8:30 p.m. in Cafe; DJ and dancing to Top 40's Thurs-
Sat from 9 p.m. downstairs in "Ribs," formerly Fred P. Ott's; $3 cover after 10 p.m.

Cityside, South Canopy, 742-7390
11 a.m.-12:30 a.m. Mon-Wed, to 2 a.m. Thurs-Sun; $3 cover Fri & Sat after 8:30 p.m.
Guitarist Sun-Wed; live rock band Thurs-Sat from 9 p.m.; feel free to dance
even though there's no dance floor.

Serendipity 3, South Market, street level, 523-2339
9 a.m.-11:30 p.m. Mon-Thurs, to midnight Fri, Sat & Sun
Live blues bands Sundays 9 p.m-midnight with free buffet.

Seaside Restaurant & Bar, South Market, street level, 742-8728
9 a.m.-9:30 p.m. Sun-Wed, to 12:30 a.m. Thurs, to 1:30 a.m. Fri & Sat
You can dance here if you get the urge, but you will have to keep
feeding the juke box to feel the beat.

Houlihan's, 60 State St, (edge of Market) 367-6377
11:30 a.m.-2 a.m. 7 days; food served to 11 p.m. Mon-Thurs, to 12 Fri & Sat, to 10:30 Sun
Cover after 8 p.m. Fri, Sat ($5) and Sun ($3); $2 off parking at 75 State St garage
Casual, charismatic and crowded; DJ and dancing nightly starting at 6:30 p.m.

BLUES IN THE NIGHT - BLUES CLUBS

Blues and jazz fans do not recognize any cultural or age barriers; therefore all of the clubs featuring these forms of music are patronized by the
most heterogeneous crowds found anywhere else. The younger set,
however, has earmarked some as their own, and those are noted.

Sticky Mike's Blues Bar, Boylston Pl, 351-2540 (Theatre District)
9 p.m.-2 a.m. Tues-Sat; cover $3 Tues-Thurs, $5 Fri & Sat
Sounds of the Mississippi Delta live every night; a cozy nightspot for blues
lovers who like to do their toe tapping at their bar stools (only bar
seating, no dance floor but dancing is allowed and encouraged).

Harper's Ferry, 158 Brighton Ave, Allston, 254-9743
To 2 a.m. nightly
Considered "home of Boston's best live R&B;" dance to local and national
acts seven nights a week in a sprawling club that holds nearly 350, mainly
in their 20's & 30's.

Midway Cafe, 3496 Washington St, Jamaica Plain, 524-9038
Looks like a '50s-style diner, sounds like a blues club - live bands Tues-Sat
10 p.m.-2 a.m.; blues jam Sun; $2 cover; dancing.

The Yard Rock, 132 East Howard St, Quincy, 472-9383
Live blues bands 9:30 p.m.-1 a.m. Wed-Sat, big band Sun 2-6 p.m.
Not to be confused with The Hard Rock, which you won't after one visit to
this homey, neighborhood club that once catered to the workers from the
scuttled Fore River Ship Yard across the street. Now a much more diverse
clientele listens (and dances to) the best in local and national acts; cover varies.

Linwood Grill, 69 Kilmarnock St, 267-8644 (near Fenway Park)
Live bands Thurs-Sat 10 p.m.-2 a.m.; a neighborhood bar with a pool
table and a juke box the rest of the week; cover $3

House of Blues, 96 Winthrop St, Cambridge, 491-2583 (off Harvard Square)
11:30 a.m.-1 a.m. Mon-Wed, food to 11; to 2 a.m. Thurs-Sat, food to midnight
$2 off parking charge at Charles Hotel garage; cover $5-$12
A well-worn townhouse looking very much like a Bourbon Street, New
Orleans juke joint; top-notch local and national talent; Cajun food; lots of
Haaavard types here.

ALL THAT JAZZ - JAZZ CLUBS

Wally's Cafe, 427 Mass. Ave, 424-1408 (near Symphony Hall)
9 p.m.-2 a.m. nightly
Jazz at its jazziest in a setting synergetic with jazz - small, smokey, a bit
dingy and crowded; Boston's oldest jazz club (47 years) where the blend
of ebony and ivory extends to the patrons as well as the music; a must
stop for the brothers Marselis whenever they are in town as well as other
jazz legends. Word is out, however, that Wally's is floundering and may
not be around much longer.

Johnny D's Uptown, 17 Holland St, Somerville (Davis Square), 776-2004
Live music and dancing nightly from 8:30 p.m.-1 a.m; Monday is Cajun
night—Cajun music and free dance lessons; food; a hip nightspot only a
hop from the city; cover varies (from $7)

Sculler's Jazz Club, Guest Quarters Suite Hotel, 400 Soldiers Field Rd, Brighton, 783-0811
8:30 p.m.-1 a.m. Mon-Sat; cover varies; valet parking $3
Good jazz in a more refined setting where the patrons applaud politely, yet enthusiastically, rather than hooting out their approval of the local and national performers featured there.

Middle East Restaurant, 472 Mass. Ave, Cambridge, 354-8238
Restaurant: A small space with live music nightly 7 p.m.-1 a.m.; cover $5-$7
Club: Dark and spacious with live music nightly - 9 p.m. to 1 a.m. Sun-Wed, to 2 a.m. Thurs-Sat; cover $6-$7; sometimes features underground alternative bands.
Bakery cafe: Belly dancer Wed nights; no cover

Regattabar, Charles Hotel, 1 Bennett St, 937-4020 (off Harvard Square)
Shows: 8:30 p.m.-9:40 p.m. Mon-Thurs, 8-9:10 & 10-11:10 Fri & Sat; $5-$19.50
The hot sounds of the national talent showcased here weekly sometimes threaten to blow out the floor-to-ceiling windows overlooking Charles Square.

Ryles, 212 Hampshire St, Cambridge, 876-9330 (Inman Square)
7 p.m.-1 a.m. Sun-Wed, to 2 a.m. Thurs-Sat; music starts at 8:30; cover $3-$7
Pick your pleasure here from two floors, each offering local, very talented talent.

Willow Jazz Club, 699 Broadway, Somerville, 623-9874 (Ball Square)
Live jazz 9 p.m.-1 a.m. nightly; a local saloon turned jazz club drawing crowds from Boston and all the "boonies."

MAKE 'EM LAUGH - COMEDY CLUBS

Dick Doherty's Comedy Vault, 124 Boylston St, (downstairs from Remington's) 267-6626
Fri & Sat 9:30 p.m. ($10); Valet $8; cash only
Features New England's stand-up and improv comedy talents in a smoke-free environment; described in the Boston press as "The Godfather of Boston Comedy."

Comedy Campus, 109 Brookline Ave (in Aku Aku) 267-6626
Valet $4; cash only

Another Dick Doherty club that offers open mike night on Thurs at 9 p.m., $6 cover; regular performances on Fri & Sat at 9 p.m., $8 cover.

Comedy Connection, Faneuil Hall Marketplace, 248-9700
Validated parking at 75 State $3
Shows: Sun at 7 p.m., Mon-Wed at 8 p,m,, Thurs at 8:30 p.m., Fri & Sat at 8 & 10:15 p.m.; tickets $6-$50;
Rated by USA Today as the "Best Comedy Club in America," certainly Boston's largest with 500 seats.

Nick's Comedy Stop, 100 Warrenton St (Theatre District), 482-0930
8:30 p.m. nightly with second show Fri & Sat at 10:30 p.m.; $6 Mon-Wed, $8 Sun & Thurs, $10 Fri, $12 Sat.
The likes of Jay Leno and Gilbert Gottfried have pulled out all the stops here in their less-famous days and return on occasion along with equally talented but not yet as well known national and local acts.

Catch a Rising Star, 661-0167
Closed at this writing, with plans to reopen in Sept '94 in Harvard Square

Daisy Buchanan's, 240A Newbury St (Back Bay) 247-8516
10 p.m.-1 a.m. Wed, free
Professional comics looking for their break at the big time.

Silhouette Lounge, 200 Brighton Ave, Allston, 254-9306
Sunday nights, free
A showcase for both professionals and amateurs.

The Kels, 161 Brighton Ave, Allston, 782-9082
10 p.m.-1 a.m. Mon, free

Lyric Stage, 140 Clarendon St, 437-7172
Fri at 10:30 p.m. October-May, $8
Gay improvisational comedy by the "Naked Brunch Comedy Troupe."

ALTERNATIVE LIFESTYLES - For gentlemen who prefer gentlemen and fem to fem

Luxor/Jox/Mario's, 69 Church St, (Bay Village, Back Bay) 423-6969
4 p.m.-1 a.m. nightly; validated parking
Favored by collegiates, jocks and combinations thereof; music videos mainly top 40's interspersed with comedy and "Best of Stage and Screen" on Tuesdays; Wednesday is 18+ night (18 to enter, 21 to drink); food in Mario's; downstairs is Jox, a sports/video bar (videos are closed captioned for the hearing impaired).

Bobby's, 69 Canal St, (North Station) 248-9520
9 p.m.-2 a.m. nightly; $3 cover Wed-Sun
DJ; dancing; drag show every Wed; Tues, Fri & Sat earmarked for women, but gentlemen not excluded; favored by the bridge & tunnel crowd.

Boston Eagle, 520 Tremont St, 542-4494
3 p.m.-2 a.m. Mon-Fri, opens at 1 p.m. Sat and at noon on Sun; cash only
A neighborhood bar for the Levi and T-shirt crowd, who do a takeoff on the Marlboro Man, only tougher; last stop in nightly rounds for the last chance.

Campus, 21 Brookline Ave (Fenway), 864-0400
9 p.m.-2 a.m. Wed-Sat; cover $3
The other side of Man-Ray, popular with gay men, mainly the college crowd (18+); house music and dancing.

Chaps, 27 Huntington Ave (Back Bay), 266-7778
1 p.m.-2 a.m. 7 days; cover $2-$5, none on Mon & Thurs; cash only
Men taking showers in the midst of the dance floor (Sun), drag queens undulating on swings— just another night out with the boys; amateur strippers contest Mondays with $50 cash prizes; Tues—Oldies, Wed—Latino, Thurs, Fri, Sat—house/dance music; patrons range in age from 25-50; Men's Room—quieter, smokey side of Chaps.

Club Cafe/Moonshine, 209 Columbus Ave (So. End), 536-0966
5:30 p.m.-1 a.m. Sun-Wed, to 2 a.m. Thurs-Sat
Upscale restaurant/video/piano bar known by its critics (who keep coming

back anyway) as "Club Attitude;" snaking your way through the maze of briefcases belonging to the three-piece suit (if only in mentality), business crowd comes with the territory; continental food from $7-$20; pianist/singer Wed-Sat 8-11; special events in **Moonshine**, located in rear.

Fritz Lounge, 26 Chandler St, (South End) 482-4428
Noon-2 a.m. 7 days; cash only
A softball players' hangout, great for a pre-Chaps cocktail or on Sundays starting at 5.

Jacques, 79 Broadway St (Bay Village) 426-8902
8:30 p.m.-midnight; cover $3 weekdays, $5 weekends; shows starting at 10:30 p.m.
Some born females would kill to look as good as some of the transvestites and female impersonators here, struttin' their stuff in a '50s-style drag show everyone would enjoy. Decor is so '70s, it's back in again.

Napoleon Club, 52 Piedmont St (Bay Village), 338-7547
5 p.m.-2 a.m. everyday; cover $3 Fri & Sat; cash only
A mixed bag--a more mature but sometimes boisterous crowd on first floor usually gathered around the piano yelling suggestions to an unflappable pianist who moves with ease from one song to another as his audience drowns him out; a second piano bar in the back room on Saturdays; young, pretty boys in disco upstairs Fri & Sat dancing to anything from a Viennese waltz to Patsy Cline.

119 Merrimac St, (North Station) address same as the name, 367-0713
10:30 a.m.-2 a.m. Mon-Sat, opens at noon on Sunday
Levis and leather; need we say more? DJ most nights but usually not on Mon & Tues; no dancing.

Paradise Cafe, 180 Mass. Ave, Cambridge, 864-4130
4 p.m-1 a.m. Sun-Wed, to 2 Thurs-Sat; cover $3 after 10 Wed-Sat; cash only
Not to be confused with the Paradise on Comm Ave in Brighton; this is for hot boys, throbbing music, and a few other activities that have the Cambridge city fathers (and mothers) in an uproar; disco in basement dance

hall, floor shows and comedy upstairs; male dancers Wed & Sat; male strippers weekends; Latino night on Mon; Thurs - Women's Night.

Playland, 21 Essex St (Downtown), 338-7254
8 a.m.-2 a.m. Mon-Sat, opens at noon on Sun; cash only
A walk on the wild side - this is the "Combat Zone," with all the implications thereof; piano bar ("21" Lounge) upstairs Thurs-Sat starting at 8; jukebox always up and down; no dancing.

Ramrod, 1254 Boylston St (Fenway) 424-2986
Noon-2 a.m. 7 days; cash only; cover $2 on Sun, $4 on Mon
Leather world and dead serious about it - patrons not wearing black leather (Thurs-Sat) must pay a $1 fine *and* bare their chests in retribution; pizza and pool tournament Mon; two-step country dancing Tues 8-10 p.m., DJ after; Oldies Night Wed; progressive music with DJ Thurs-Sat; buffet starting at 8 p.m. Sun followed by DJ; dancing only on Tues & Sun.

Sporter's Cafe/Sling, 228 Cambridge St, 742-4084
3 p.m.-2 a.m. 7 days; cash only
Among the oldest gay bars in America and once strictly for the briefcase crowd, now a neighborhood, leather cruise bar with neighbors some may not choose to live next door to; a dance room, a leather room and a bar in between the two; DJ and dancing Thurs-Sun.

Quest, 1270 Boylston St, 424-7747
Mon, Queer Circus ($1), Wed, Girl Twirl ($3), Sat, Gay Saturdays ($5); usually a very young crowd; see listing under **CLUBS, Fenway.**

Venus DeMilo, 11 Lansdowne St, 421-9595
Wed—dancing to house music ($4); see listing under **CLUBS,** Fenway

Axis/DV8, 13 Lansdowne St, 262-2437
Sun—$10 for 18+, $7 for 21+; see listing under **CLUBS,** Fenway

Esmé, 3 Boylston Pl (Theatre District), 482-3399
Fem 2 Fem Sundays; see listing under **CLUBS, Theatre District**

BOSTON BY NIGHT

The Art Zone, 150 Kneeland St (Financial District), 695-0087
"Women's Club"—Dancing to the Danger Zone, Sat 10:15 p.m.-2 a.m. $5;
get $2 off on "The Morning After" Sunday brunch, advertised as "finally a
brunch for women." Plans in the works for a "Men's Club" on Fridays—call
for more info.

Paramount, 965 Mass. Ave (South End) 541-0101
Thurs (See listing under **CLUBS, South End**)

The Loft, 21 Stanhope St (Back Bay), 262-2121
An after hours (opens at 2 a.m. until 6 or 7 a.m.),
semi-private club earmarked for alternative lifestyles on Sat (see **IIN THE
WEE HOURS**).

Safari Club, 90 Wareham St (between Albany & Harrison), 292-0011
A gym if you choose to work out or a place you can merely hang out
anytime of the day or night (open 24 hours); lockers, TV lounge and
parking but no booze nor any other stuff the cops would frown on.

DINNER THEATRES

Medieval Manor Theatre Restaurant, 246 E Berkeley St (So. End), 423-4900
Parking in rear $2; Sun 6 p.m., Mon & Wed-Fri 8 p.m., Sat 5 & 9:30;
tickets $27 for Sun, Wed & Thurs, $22 Mon, $32 Fri & Sat; only by reservation
A knight to remember in the midst of a Middle Ages spoof as you feast
(and I use that word lightly) on a 6-course banquet while suffering the
slings and arrows of a tyrannical (all in fun) "king" and his court, especially if
you are seated below the salt (you'll find out what that means); 2 1/2
hours long.

Mystery Cafe Dinner Theatre, 290 Congress St (in Three Cheers Bar),
524-CAFE
Thurs 7:30 p.m., Fri 8 p.m., Sat 6 & 9 p.m., Sun 6 p.m.
Tickets $28.95-$32.95; only by reservation; free parking
Murder and mayhem along with a 4-course dinner; 2 1/2 hours long; also
a slightly abbreviated version on a two-hour cruise in Boston Harbor
spring and summer.

Rosie O'Grady's Blind Pig Saloon, 386 Market St, Brighton Center, 783-2333
7:55-11 p.m. Thurs ($21), Fri ($23) & Sat ($25)
Roaring with tales of the '20s prohibition/speakeasy era performed by Rosie and her guys and dolls as you try to finish your 4-course Mediterranean-style dinner before the "cops" raid the joint or the bad guys shoot it up.

Lombardo's Dinner Theatre, 6 William St (Kelly Square), East Boston 567-5221
Sporadically features Broadway musicals along with a three-course Italian dinner for around $32.

FOR THE ATHLETICALLY INCLINED

Jillian's Billiard Club, 145 Ipswich St, (behind Fenway Park) 437-0300
11 a.m.-2 a.m. Mon-Sat, opens at noon Sun; valet parking after 7 p.m. $5
No cigar-chomping, Runyonesque characters here (don't even think
hustler) but a right-on-cue, 20's-40's crowd playing pool (56 tables),
shuffleboard (4), ping pong (6 tables), darts (5 alleys), blackjack (5 tables)
or in the well-lit, nicely decorated, high-tech game room. Pool costs $9-$13
per hour depending on time and number of people; blackjack is $5 for
$1,000 in chips and if you win, all you get is satisfaction (gambling is not
yet allowed in Boston). Hunger attacks can be fended off in the International Cafe (pub foods).

Boston Billiard Club, 126 Brookline Ave (near Kenmore Square), 536-POOL
11 a.m.-2 a.m. daily; complimentary parking evenings and weekends
Billiards Digest rates this place "the handsdown finest room in the country."
Minnesota Fats could probably find some worthy opponents here, but the
accent is on fun, not skill. Price changes according to number of people
and time, ie; $9 per hour for two Sun-Thurs, $11 for two Fri & Sat; light menu
and an impressive list of beers and ales available at the bar (32 feet
long and always crowded).

The Golf Club, 3 Lansdowne St, (across from Fenway Park), 262-0300
5 p.m.-2 a.m. Mon-Fri, opens at 11 a.m. on Sat, noon on Sun; valet after 6 p.m. $4
An indoor miniature golf course open and ready for the most devoted
duffers all year long even though the weather outside may be frightful;
the usual twists, turns and traps with a few surprises (you play through a
cave on one hole); waterfalls, flowers and real rock formations give the
outdoorsy feeling; $6 pp per round.

Boston Paintball, 131 Beverly St (across from Boston Garden), 742-6612
Open 24 hours for reservations to play anytime
The latest rage for those who don't mind getting pelted in the true sense
of the word— participants use air-powered guns that shoot gelatin
capsules. Anyone hit is out, and no one can cheat because the capsule
explodes in a burst of color; the one left unblemished wins. If this is the

"Sport of the Nineties," I'm not sure I want to know what's on tap in the '00s. (what *will* we call the first decade of the next century?). Priced according to number of people, ie $40 pp for a group of 10 for 3 hours which includes 200 rounds of paint and all equipment.

Ryan Family Amusement Center, 64 Brookline Ave (below Fenway Park), 267-8495
11 a.m.-11 p.m. Mon-Fri, opens at 9 a.m. Sat & Sun
Enough going on to keep all in the family busy and contented—20 candlepin alleys ($1.80 per string Mon-Sat 9-5, $2 after 5 and all day Sun), 11 pool tables ($5 per hour for 2-4 players), and a game room with 20 video games.

Boston Bowl, 820 Wm. T. Morrissey Blvd, Dorchester, 825-3800
About five miles outside of the city but a good place to know about in case you can't sleep—open 24 hours daily; 50 lanes, both candlepin and tenpin ($10.95 per hour per lane), 12 pocket billiard tables ($8 per hour), game room and full service restaurant.

SEDENTARY PLEASURES

Suffolk Downs, 111 Waldemar Ave, East Boston 567-3900
On Blue Line from Government Center to Suffolk Downs stop, free shuttle bus to gate; free general parking or $2-$4 for preferred parking (closer to the gate); general admission $2, clubhouse $4; live horse races everyday but Tues & Thurs; simulcasts from tracks throughout the country most evenings; two restaurants open to public (3rd for members only).

Wonderland Dog Track, Wonderland Park, Revere, 284-1300
On Blue Line from Government Center to Wonderland; "Wonderbus" from "T" and through parking lots (free or preferred at $1); grandstand $1, clubhouse $2; dog races live or simulcast or both every afternoon (beginning at 12:25 p.m., track opens at 11 a.m) and every night (beginning at 7:25 p.m., track opens at 6 p.m.); dining room and pub.

BOSTON BY NIGHT

Foxwoods High Stakes Bingo & Casino, Rte 2, Ledyard, Connecticut,
1-800-FOXWOOD
Two-to-2 1/2 hours from Boston and as close as Boston gets to legal
gambling short of the lottery or race tracks. Owned and operated by
the Mashantucket Pequot Indian Nation and located on tribal land, the
complex offers a Casino with slot machines, keno, poker, craps, roulette,
blackjack and a few other ways to lose or win money as well as restaurants, an inn, lounges, bars and shops where you can spend your winnings
(or sulk over your losses). Daily buses available at Peter Pan Terminal
across from South Station, 1-800-237-8747, Ext. 270, 7:25 a.m. daily, return
at 3:55 p.m.; Fri & Sat 1:30 p.m. bus also available, return at 10 p.m.; $19.95
round trip Sun-Fri, $17.95 Sat.; also Entertainment Tours, (pick up at corner of
Harrison Ave and Kneeland Street, Chinatown), 10:30 a.m. daily, return at 7
p.m., $20 round trip, reservations required—617-451-3478.

IN THE WEE HOURS

As was mentioned previously, there are private after-hours clubs in Boston,
but even if I knew all of them (which I don't), listing them here would serve
no purpose since they would be moved as soon as their locations become public. Your friendly concierge or bartender may be acquainted
with one or two and may be encouraged to tell for reason or reasons
that shall be known only by you and he/she. The only one that operates
somewhat openly is **The Loft**, a semi-private club ($10 makes you a
member for the night, $8 entrance for members) on 21 Stanhope St. (262-
2121), wedged between the rear of the Hard Rock Cafe and the police
station. It opens at 2 a.m., goes strong until 6 or 7 a.m., serves only soft
drinks, designates certain nights for different crowds, ie Thurs College Night,
Fri African American and Sat Gay, although that could change without
notice. Those that show up at the door without having some connections
depend on the whim of the door person to gain entrance.

If the Loft is higher than you aspire to cap off your night or bowling is
not up your alley (see **Boston Bowl** under **ATHLETICALLY INCLINED** listing),
go for a midnight movie:

The Circle Cinema, Cleveland Circle, Brookline, 566-4040
The Allston Cinema, 214 Harvard Ave, 277-2140
Showcase Cinemas
  Dedham, Rt 1 at junction of 128, Exit 15A, 326-4955
  Woburn, Rt 128, Exit 35 and Rt. 38, 933-5330
  Revere, Rt. C1 and Squire Rd., 286-1660
  Quincy, 1585 Hancock St, 773-5700

Loews Harvard Square Theatre, 10 Church St., Cambridge, 864-4580
Fri & Sat; discounted parking in University Place Garage; also features Fri &
Sat 12:15 a.m. showings of the Rocky Horror Show complete with live cast
and bizarre costumes (and that's just the audience).

Sometimes offering late showings (check listings) are:

Somerville Loews, Assembly Square (Rt. 93 North from Boston), 628-7000

The Copley Place Theatre, 100 Huntington Ave (in Copley Place), 266-
1300
$2 parking in garage with validation after 5 p.m. until 2 a.m.

The Cheri, Dalton St, Back Bay (opposite Sheraton Boston Hotel), 536-2870
Discounted parking in adjacent garage.

BOSTON BY NIGHT

MISCELLANEOUS SERVICES

Commonwealth Laundries & Cleaners, 362 Comm. Ave. at Mass Ave, 267-7100
Same day pick up and delivery Mon-Fri 5-6:30 a.m., 11 a.m.-1 p.m., 6-8
p.m.; 10-lb minimum $1.25 per pound washed, dried and folded; shirts $1.35;
suits $8.05; pants/skirts $4.15.

Takeout Taxi, 277-4440
5 p.m.-10 p.m. Sun-Wed, to 10:30 Thurs-Sat
Order dinner from a variety of restaurants such as Charley's Saloon,
Zuma's, Atlantic Fish Co; $3.95 plus cost of food; serves all of Boston,
Brookline and some suburbs.

Late Night, All Night

Pizza Market, 100 Topeka St (off So. Hampton), 541-9377
Free delivery 11 a.m-3 a.m; home of the 24" pizza

La Mamma Pizza and More, 190 Brighton Ave, Brighton, 783-1661
Free delivery to closing at 1 a.m. to Brighton, Allston and Brookline;
empanadas, seafood, pasta, chicken, calzones and pizza.

Aku-Aku, 109 Brookline Ave (Fenway) 536-0420
Szechuan and Cantonese food delivered throughout Boston until 1:45 a.m. nightly.

Buzzy's Fabulous Roast Beef, 327 Cambridge St, 523-4896
Open 7:30 a m-5:00 a m for not-so-fabulous roast beef or pepper-steak
sanwiches, but they sure taste good after a night of revelry.

International House of Pancakes, 850 Soldiers Field Rd, Brighton, 787-0533—
24 hours all week; 500 Commonwealth Ave, 859-0458—to 3 a.m. all week

Katz's Bagel Bakery, 139 Park St, Chelsea 884-9738
To 2 a.m. Fri & Sat—a bagel, a little cream cheese, some lox, and heaven awaits.

Star Market, 800 Boylston St, Back Bay (in the Prudential Center) and
33 Kilmarnock St, Fenway; full-service 24-hour super markets

Golden Goose, 179 Commercial St (on the waterfront)
To 2 a.m Sun-Thurs, all night Fri & Sat
Full line of groceries, sandwiches and hot foods; also videos and firewood
for those who feel an insominia attack coming on.

24-Hour Mini Marts
Christy's, 243 Dartmouth St, Back Bay; 55 Berkeley St, So. End;
425 Brookline Ave, Fenway
7-11 Stores, 64 Charles St, Beacon Hill; Corner of Commercial & Hanover
Sts, No. End

CVS Pharmacy, 155 Charles St, 523-1028 (pharmacy), 227-0437 (front store)
At the base of Beacon Hill; open 24 hours except the pharmacy (to midnight).

24-Hour Pharmacies closest to Boston
CVS, 35 White St, (Porter Square) Cambridge, 876-5519
Walgreens, 757 Gallivan Boulevard, Dorchester, 282-5246

24-hour service stations:
Fenway Service Center (Exxon), 1420 Boylston St, 247-8942
Merit Station, 219 Cambridge St, Allston, 254-9488

Flying Locksmiths, 1-800-649-KEYS; covers all areas within 495 belt;
makes new keys on the spot; on call 24 hours.

Emergency Towing Services:
AAA, 1-800-222-4357
Downtown Boston Towing, 345-0818; for those without the red, white
and blue card

24-Hour Copy Shops
Copy Cop: 815 Boylston St, Back Bay 267-9267
260 Washington St, Downtown 367-3370
1295 Beacon St, Brookline 371-6775

Kinko's: 187 Dartmouth St, Back Bay 262-6188
111 Western Ave., Brighton 491-2859
10 Post Office Sq., Downtown 482-4400

24-Hour Animal Hospitals
Angell Memorial, 350 S. Huntington Ave, Fenway, 522-7282
Brookline Animal Hosp., 678 Brookline Ave, 277-2030

Lost Credit Cards
Mastercard/Visa, 1-800-336-8472
Diners Club/Carte Blanche, 1-800-525-9135
American Express, 1-800-528-2121
Discover/Private Issue—1-800-347-2683

TRANSPORTATION

The country's first subway system, The Massachusetts Bay Transportation Authority (MBTA), commonly called The "T," provides clean, efficient, safe and fast subway, bus and streetcar service throughout the Greater Boston area and suburbs between 5 a.m. and 12:45 a.m. Fares vary depending on your destination, but 85 cents (the cost of a token) will take you throughout the core city and beyond. Maximum fare is $2 to the farthest point. If boarding on the street where there are no token booths, be prepared with the exact change (no bills). The "T" offers a Visitor Passport giving unlimited travel in Boston for three days at $9 or seven days at $18, as well as discounts on popular attractions. Call the "Ts" Customer Service Center, 722-3200 for more information. See the specially designed "T" map on the next page for directions to areas addressed in this book.

Free shuttle buses transport from all Logan Airport terminals to the Airport "T" Station on the Blue Line, just two stops to the Waterfront and three to Government Center. Since much of The "T" service is still not accessible for the physically impaired (they're working on it), a special-needs van is available to anyplace within the area covered by The "T" at the same cost, but one must apply in advance to qualify, providing necessary documentation of need (a one-time process for all future use). This generally takes two weeks. Anyone accompanying the qualified rider may also board. Arrangements for a ride must be made 4-5 days in advance. Call 722-5123 or 1-800-533 MBTA.

Boston's taxis are among the least expensive in the country ($1.50 for the first quarter mile, 20 cents for each eighth mile after that). There are 1,565 licensed cabs, about 40 of which are handicapped accessible. Most drivers are courteous, knowledgeable, neat and adhere to Boston's "dress code" calling for a tidy appearance (no tank tops, sweatsuits, sandals, etc.). Cabs can be found at the many stands throughout the city, particularly in front of all of Boston's hotels, called (consult the Yellow pages under Taxicabs), or flagged.

Several dozen limousine services operate in Boston, generally round the clock, for around $50-$60 an hour for a four-hour minimum (a tip for the driver is also expected but not added to the tab). Most also provide service to and from the airport, train and bus stations or other destinations for flat rates depending on the distance. One limo service, Waites Transportation, 567-5867, also offers round-the-clock plane rentals from a single-engine (around $200 per hour) to a jet (from $2,500 per hour).

AND, when all is said and done, and Boston still doesn't have enough action or excitement to suit your tastes, you can charter a jet plane to New York (or anywhere else in the world) any time of the day or night through Jet Aviation Business Jets (Hanscom Field, Bedford, 1-800-Rent-Jet). For only $12,144, you and 11 of your nearest and dearest can fly off to the "Big Apple" and return (within 24 Hours) in a Gulf Stream, two pilot, twin engine jet with a flight attendant who serves drinks and snacks. Personally, I'll stick with Boston. I love Boston, and so will you when you get to know the city as well as I do.

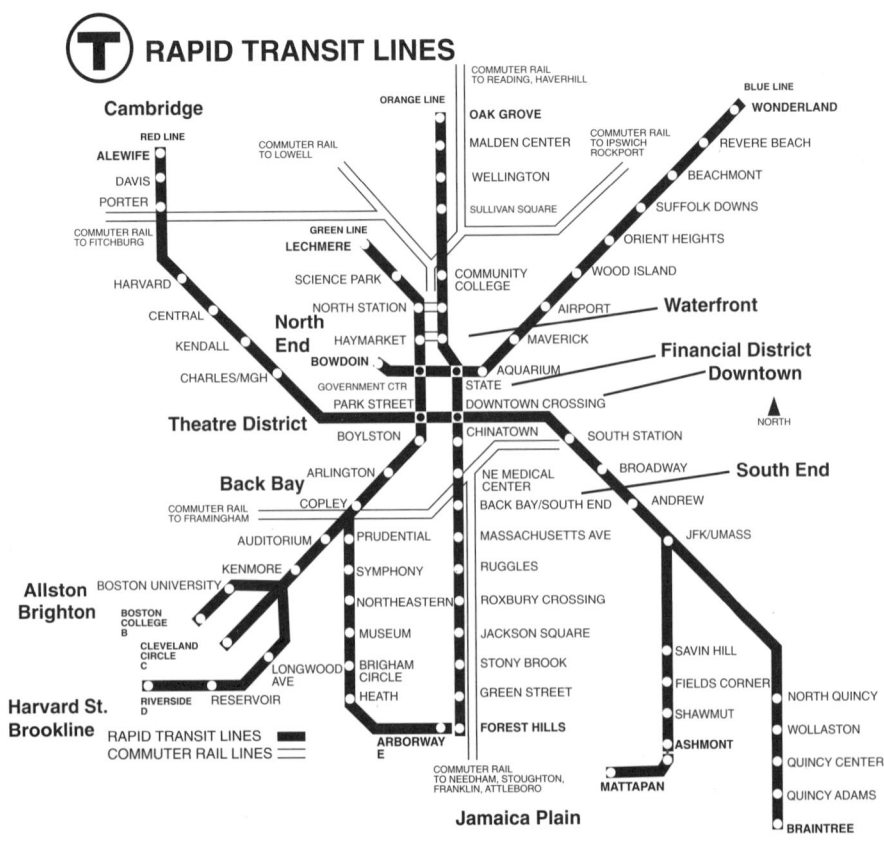